The 500 Hidden Secrets of

AMSTERDAM

D1381867

INTRODUCTION

This is a guide to the Amsterdam that almost no one knows.
It takes you off the beaten track to discover the city's hidden gardens,
unknown museums and small coffee bars. Within these pages, you
will find the five places to eat the best *bitterballen*, five of the most
crooked canal houses and five of the best independent bookstores.

The aim is to take the reader to unexpected places that are different in
some way from the obvious tourist destinations. This book encourages
you to set out to find a 1950s Russian submarine, a Maria altar in
a hotel garden, or secretly placed statues by an anonymous sculptor.
You will also be guided to a restaurant located in a former pirate radio
station, through a museum alley that houses a 17th-century giant,
and into a cinema located in an old pathological anatomy laboratory.

If you want to experience some of Amsterdam's more unusual sides,
this is the perfect guide for you. Visit a secret 'clandestine church'
in the middle of the red light district, venture out of the city centre
to sample the best Indonesian cuisine, or try some homemade 'jenever'
at a distillery that's deeply hidden in a park.

This book doesn't mention everything there is to see in the city.
There are already enough guidebooks and websites that cover the
familiar sights. The aim was to create an intimate guide to the places
the authors would recommend to a friend who wants to discover
the real Amsterdam.

HOW TO
USE THIS BOOK?

This book contains 500 things about Amsterdam in 100 different categories. Some are places to visit, others are random bits of information. The aim is to inspire, not to cover the city from A to Z.

The places listed in the guide are given an address, a district and a number. The district and number allow you to find the locations on the maps at the beginning of the book. The maps are not detailed enough to navigate around the city, but you can pick up a good city map at one of the 'I amsterdam' Visitor Centres – either at the Stationsplein, directly across from Central Station, or at Amsterdam Airport Schiphol (Holland Tourist Information), by Schiphol Plaza at Arrivals 2. Or the addresses can be located on a smartphone.

Please also bear in mind that cities change all the time. The chef who hits a high note one day may be uninspiring on the day you happen to visit. The bar considered one of the 5 best places for live music might be empty on the night you visit. This is obviously a highly personal selection. You might not always agree with it. If you want to leave a comment, recommend a bar or reveal your favourite secret place, please visit the website *www.the500hiddensecrets.com* or follow *@500hiddensecrets* on Instagram or Facebook and leave a comment.

THE AUTHORS

Saskia Naafs and Guido van Eijck are writers and journalists. They specialise in a wide range of topics, from politics and urban planning, to education and housing. They write for weekly *De Groene Amsterdammer* and a local online magazine called *Vers Beton*. They are also the authors of *The 500 Hidden Secrets of Rotterdam* and *Hidden Holland*. Their work takes them into the far corners of their capital city, to places they probably wouldn't have discovered otherwise.

Having lived in Amsterdam for more than a decade, Saskia finds that every neighbourhood has its own charm. It's a shame that most tourists never venture out of the city centre, therefore you will find quite a few addresses outside the famous canal belt. Having said that, even the old canal houses have their 'secrets'. Just look closely at the old houses, their richly decorated facades, the crooked windows, and the colourful gable stones.

Guido recommends anyone visiting Amsterdam to explore the North. Once called the 'Siberia of Amsterdam', it's now a thriving, humming place. Take the ferry to the old shipyards at NDSM, visit the old worker's houses in Tuindorp Oostzaan, or leisurely stroll the Nieuwendammerdijk, and don't forget to stop halfway for one of the best pieces of apple pie in Amsterdam.

The authors wish to thank their friends, family, colleagues and acquaintances for offering invaluable tips about the city. Without their precious help, it would have been impossible to draw up a list of so many places, some of which tourists have never heard of, some of which even born and bred *Amsterdammers* don't know. They would also like to thank publisher Luster for their excellent guidance and advice. And last but not least, they would like to thank photographer Tino van den Berg for his good company and for beautifully capturing the essence of Amsterdam.

AMSTERDAM

overview

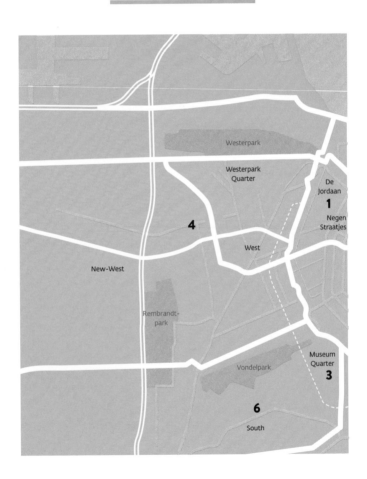

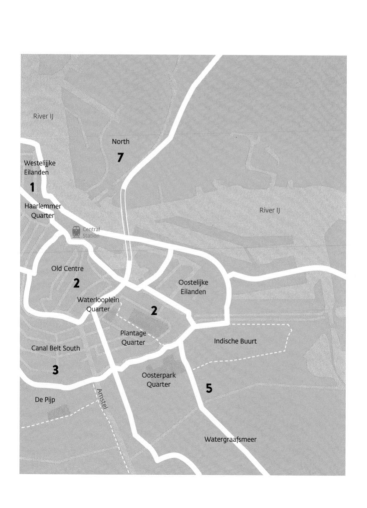

River IJ

North

7

Westelijke
Eilanden

1

Haarlemmer
Quarter

Central
Station

River IJ

Old Centre

2

Waterlooplein
Quarter

2

Oostelijke
Eilanden

Canal Belt South

3

Plantage
Quarter

Indische Buurt

De Pijp

Amstel

Oosterpark
Quarter

5

Watergraafsmeer

Map 1
WESTELIJKE EILANDEN
HAARLEMMER QUARTER

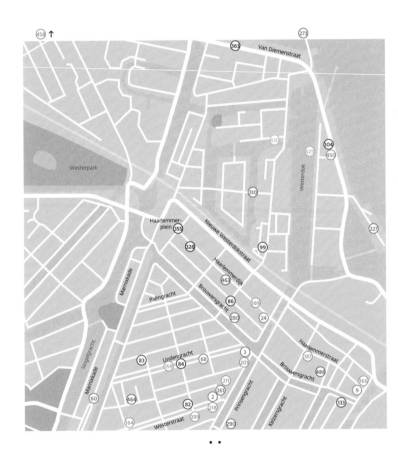

DE JORDAAN
NEGEN STRAATJES

..

Map 2
OLD CENTRE
WATERLOOPLEIN QUARTER

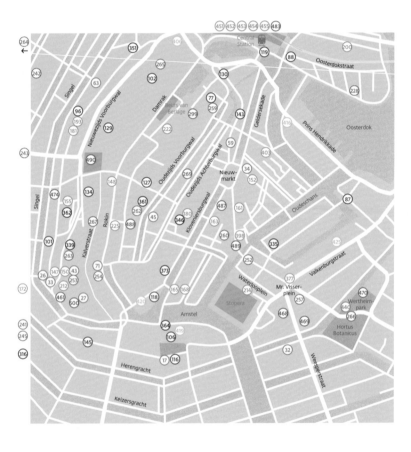

OOSTELIJKE EILANDEN
PLANTAGE QUARTER

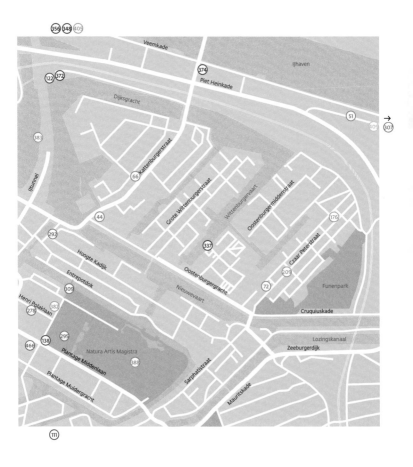

Map 3
CANAL BELT SOUTH
MUSEUM QUARTER
DE PIJP

Map 4
WEST
WESTERPARK QUARTER
NEW-WEST

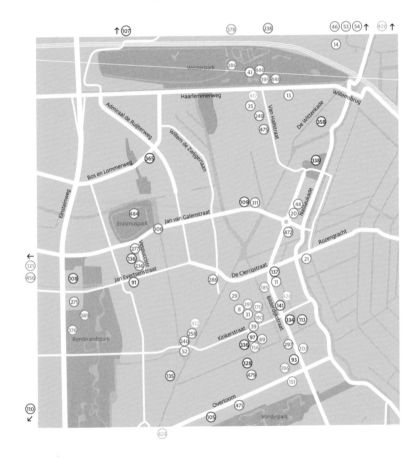

EAT — **DRINK** — SHOP — **BUILDINGS** — DISCOVER — **CULTURE** — CHILDREN — SLEEP — WEEKEND — **RANDOM**

Map 5
OOSTERPARK QUARTER
INDISCHE BUURT
WATERGRAAFSMEER

Map 6
SOUTH

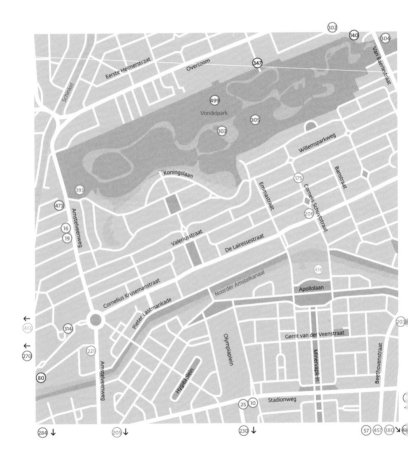

Map 7
NORTH

Ringweg Noord

Slochterweg

IJdoornlaan

IJdoornlaan

(291)
(247)

(311)
(318) (215)
(125)
Klaprozenweg
Kamperfoelieweg
(216)
(123)
(499)
Mosveld
(18)
(67)
(235) (49)
(226) (94) (289)
(198)
(78) (274)

Nieuwe Leeuwarderweg

Nieuwe Purmerweg

(256)
(1) Nieuwendammerdijk
(437) W.H.
Vliegenbos
(276)
(331)
(360)

IJtunnel

Java-eiland

River IJ

→
(415)
(234)

(157)

DE CULINAIRE WERKPLAATS

75 PLACES
TO EAT OR BUY
GOOD FOOD

The 5 best places to eat
DELICIOUS APPLE PIE

---

1 **CAFÉ 'T SLUISJE**
Nieuwendammer-
dijk 297
North ⑦
+31 (0)20 636 17 12
www.cafehetsluisje.nl

This is the perfect stop while discovering Amsterdam North. And not just because they serve large slices of apple pie, tasting of fresh and juicy apples instead of just sugar. The patio offers a view of one of the oldest locks and dikes in the city. Café 't Sluisje (meaning 'the lock') opened in 1904. The building dates from the 16th century and used to be a coffee house.

2 **WINKEL 43**
Noordermarkt 43
De Jordaan ①
+31 (0)20 623 02 23
www.winkel43.nl

Winkel 43 is a household name among apple pie lovers. Their crust is superb, the slices are huge. From Winkel's basement comes a constant stream of freshly baked apple pies. Mondays and Saturdays (market days in Noordermarkt and Westerstraat) can be especially busy. On these days, Winkel 43 offers breakfast from 7 am.

1 CAFE 'T SLUISJE

3 CAFÉ 'T PAPENEILAND

Prinsengracht 2
De Jordaan ①
+31 (0)20 624 19 89
www.papeneiland.nl

Huh? Does this age-old pub (dating from 1642) and national monument in the Jordaan area really serve apple pie? Yes, they certainly do. It's homemade, fresh, and delicious. Even Bill Clinton had a piece of apple pie at Café 't Papeneiland when he visited the Amsterdam canals in 2011.

4 KOFFIEHUIS DE HOEK

Prinsengracht 341
Old Centre ②
+31 (0)20 625 38 72

A truly old-fashioned Dutch coffee bar. It has amazingly hot drip coffee, chequered table-cloths on the tables, and pancakes and fried eggs sunny side up on the menu. They also serve a tasty and crunchy apple pie, with a sprinkling of almonds on top. On sunny days, their terrace on the canals is a welcome bonus.

5 PATISSERIE KUYT

Utrechtsestraat
109-111
Canal Belt South ③
+31 (0)20 623 48 33
www.patisseriekuyt.nl

Kuyt opened in 1974 in Utrechtsestraat and is renowned for its excellent *appelschnitt*, a pastry with apple, currants, raisins, almonds and cinnamon. In fact, all the cakes and biscuits in this pastry shop are a visual treat. Visit their tearoom next door, where you can sit down and order sweet and savoury morsels.

The 5 best
FRESH BAKERIES

---

6 **BAKING LAB**
Linnaeusstraat 99
Oosterpark Q ⑤
+31 (0)20 240 01 58
www.bakinglab.nl

Baking Lab is an experimental bakery and lunchroom. Jechiam Gural quit his job in IT to become a professional baker in 2017. He likes to explore old and new techniques, using old grains and turning stale croissants into veggie bacon for instance. He also organises workshops.

7 **BAKKERIJ HARTOG**
Wibautstraat 77
Oosterpark Q ⑤
+31 (0)20 220 00 44
www.volkorenbrood.nl

Aagje Hartog was known for her wholemeal bread when she was still living in the province of Friesland, in the late 19th century. When people from Amsterdam discovered her *volkorenbrood*, they persuaded the Hartog family to sell their products in the capital. They eventually moved to the Jordaan quarter, and later to Ruyschstraat in the eastern part of the city.

8 BAKKERIJ STRAATHOF

Ten Katestraat 21
West ④
+31 (0)20 612 97 09
*www.bakkerij
straathof.nl*

You can only find the bread of this family-owned bakery at the lively Ten Kate market, which is held daily. The bakery is just behind the market stall, guaranteeing a constant supply of crusty fresh (sourdough) bread, croissants and cakes.

9 STADSBAKKER JONGEJANS

Haarlemmerstraat 4
Haarlemmer Q ①
+31 (0)20 624 76 11
*www.bakker
jongejans.nl*

The first branch of this family business opened in the 1920s and is currently run by the fifth generation of bakers. The muesli buns (called *Amsterdammertjes*) are definitely worth a try, as is the rest of the assortment. Jongejans also sells homemade chocolate paste, jams and peanut butter.

10 LE FOURNIL DE SÉBASTIEN

Olympiaplein 119
South ⑥
+31 (0)20 672 42 11
www.lefournil.nl

The French baker Sébastien de Roturier doesn't trust Dutch colleagues who suddenly start to sell French bread. That's because they lack the expertise, he says, just as he lacks the expertise to bake Dutch bread. De Roturier started his own bakery in 2006, in Amsterdam South, and it's the best place to go for freshly baked, French-style bread without additives. Just look at the long queue if you don't believe us.

The 5 best places to eat
VEGETARIAN FOOD

---

11 **MEATLESS DISTRICT**
Bilderdijkstraat 65-67
West ④
+31 (0)20 722 08 04
www.meatless
district.com

Meatless District is a 100% vegan restaurant with a menu that changes with the seasons. It serves lunch, snacks, diner, and breakfast on the weekend. Think tasty pastas, salads and burgers, among others. They also have a good beer selection.

12 **BETTY'S**
Rijnstraat 75
Canal Belt South ③
+31 (0)20 644 58 96
www.bettys.nl

Betty's has been the to go to vegetarian restaurants for several years. The owners Guido and Lien cook without fish, meat or eggs and vegan or gluten free on request. They offer a three-course surprise menu. For dessert, you can choose from one of the terrific cakes baked by Lien. They also have a store where they sell their favourite products, like chili powder from Mexico's rainforest or French grape seed oil.

13 DE CULINAIRE WERKPLAATS

Fannius Scholten-
straat 10
Westerpark Q ④
+31 (0)6 546 46 576
www.deculinaire
werkplaats.nl

At this culinary workshop, they make edible works of art with vegetables, fruits and grains. The owners Marjolein and Eric derive inspiration from different themes, such as a colour, a landscape, architecture or the Golden Age. The menu is made up of five small, exquisitely presented dishes. There is no set price: after having finished your dinner, you decide what the food was worth. Only open on Fridays and Saturdays.

14 DOPHERT

Spaarndammer-
straat 49
Westerpark Q ④
+31 (0)20 752 05 81
www.dophert
catering.nl

A vegan breakfast and lunchroom with a laidback hipster vibe in the up and coming Spaarndammerstraat. Try their gluten-free sandwiches with pumpkin hummus or tofu scramble, or a piece of their delicious vegan carrot cake. Every first Thursday of the month they organise a dinner as well. Book ahead.

15 MARITS EETKAMER

Andreas Bonn-
straat 34
Oosterpark Q ⑤
+31 (0)20 776 38 64
www.marits
eetkamer.nl

On Fridays and Saturdays, Marit cooks the most fabulous vegetarian dishes and serves them up in her own living room. It's like going over to a friend's house for dinner, but someone who can actually cook, and without having to help with the dishes. Choose from a three or four-course menu. The flavours are pure and fresh, the products are mostly organic or fair-trade, and locally sourced.

The 5 best places for traditional
INDONESIAN FOOD

16 BLAUW

Amstelveenseweg
158-160
South ⑥
+31 (0)20 675 50 00
www.restaurant
blauw.nl

Traditional Indonesian cuisine with a modern twist. In the bright red interior, tables are closely packed together which makes for a cosy atmosphere. Dutch people like to order a so-called *rijsttafel* (rice table) here, which is a combination of many small dishes. Order the meat, fish or vegetarian option. For dessert try the *es ketan hitam*, a black rice pudding with ice-cream and coconut milk.

17 INDRAPURA

Rembrandtplein 42
Old Centre ②
+31 (0)20 623 73 29
indrapura.nl

Indrapura is located in busy Rembrandt-plein and is famous for its *rijsttafel*: fill your table with an abundance of tasty (sometimes spicy!) Indonesian dishes. They offer a 25% discount for early birds who finish and pay before 8 pm. Try a slice of *spekkoek* (traditional layered cake) for dessert.

18 KANNIBALEN EN PARADIJSVOGELS

Van der Pekstraat 91
North ⑦
+31 (0)20 370 03 48
www.kannibalen
enparadijsvogels.nl

No *wayang* puppets or *sarongs* in this modern and fresh take on the traditional Indonesian *toko*. This friendly neighbourhood restaurant prepares everything fresh on the spot – and you can really taste the difference. They serve all the classics and even have a vegan rice table option.

19 TOKO KOK KITA

Amstelveenseweg 166
South ⑥
+31 (0)20 670 29 33
www.kokkita.nl

If you are not in the mood for sitting down in the somewhat formal Indonesian restaurant Blaauw in Amstelveenseweg, you can join the line in front of the nearby Toko Kok Kita. Their take-away rice tables, *sambal goreng* spicy beans, and lamb *sate kambing* are definitely worth the wait.

20 JUN

Frederik Hendrik-
straat 98
West ④
+31 (0)20 785 91 85
www.restaurantjun.nl

The decor is simple, but all the more attention goes out to the food. Jun serves classic Indonesian dishes like *soto ayam* and *rendang*, but also has lesser known dishes on the menu like *Ikan woku-woku* (sea bass in red sauce) and *Tongseng sapi* (tenderloin Yogyakarta style). Chef Edy Junaedy changes the menu every three months.

The 5 best places to buy
CHEESE

---

21 FROMAGERIE ABRAHAM KEF

Marnixstraat 192
West ④
+31 (0)20 420 00 97
www.abrahamkef.nl

You'll gladly make the extra effort to go to Kef. It's a traditional cheese shop that's been around for over sixty years. Kef specialises in French cheese, but actually sells cheeses from all over Europe. On Sundays, they organise cheese and wine tastings. New branches opened in the northern (Van der Pekplein 1B) and eastern (Czaar Peterstraat 137) parts of the city.

22 DE KAASKAMER

Runstraat 7
Negen Straatjes ①
+31 (0)20 623 34 83
www.kaaskamer.nl

This is what heaven must look like for cheese lovers. The Kaaskamer is stocked to the hilt with round, yellow hard cheeses. They come in all varieties, like a farmer's Gouda with truffle, or an old sheep's cheese with sea lavender. There are between 300 to 400 different types. Try the cheese on a fresh baguette, or just take it home in a big chunk.

24 KAASLAND

23 KAASHUIS TROMP

Utrechtsestraat 90
Canal Belt South ③
+31 (0)20 624 13 99
www.kaashuistromp.nl

Henk Kol runs this store that's open seven days a week, located near a good butcher, a patisserie and a fish monger. This really is the place to go to for foodies. The shop serves delicious freshly-made sandwiches on rustic bread and sells Dutch and European cheeses.

24 KAASLAND

Haarlemmerdijk 1
Haarlemmer Q ①
+31 (0)20 625 79 45
www.kaasland.eu

The first thing you see when entering this store is a mountain of cheese, with different tasting platters sticking out. Kaasland sells different hard Dutch cheeses, but it has a particularly good selection of French cheese as well. Besides that, it also sells scrumptious bread, freshly-roasted nuts and dried fruit. It's really not hard not to leave this store with two full bags.

25 L'AMUSE

Olympiaplein 111
South ⑥
+31 (0)20 672 76 70
www.lamuse.nl

The owners of l'Amuse have an encyclopaedic knowledge of cheese and are always looking for new ways to present and pair cheese (with tea, whisky or sake for example). They provide recipes on their website, give tips on how to create the perfect cheese board, and they organise tastings.

The 5 best places for
FRENCH FRIES

---

26 PATATSTEEG
Heisteeg 3
Old Centre ②
+31 (0)20 422 64 47

Patatsteeg is located in a little side alley of Spuistraat and sells freshly sliced French fries in large or very large portions. On the outside their fries are golden brown and crunchy, while the inside is perfectly soft. They opened a second branch in the little building on the bridge between Stadionkade and Parnassusweg, in Amsterdam South.

27 VLAAMS FRITESHUIS VLEMINCKX
Voetboogstraat 31
Old Centre ②
+31 (0)6 547 87 000
www.vleminckx desausmeester.nl

There's probably not one tourist guide that doesn't at least mention Friteshuis Vleminckx. So why call it a hidden secret then? Well, partly because if you didn't know it was there you could easily miss it but mostly because tourists, Amsterdammers and everyone else will agree that Vleminckx's fries (as well as the mayonnaise) are just fabulous.

28 VITA'S FRIET
Dappermarkt
Oosterpark Q ⑤
www.vita-friet.nl

A good way to end your visit to Dappermarkt is to order some fries at Vita's Friet. It was awarded the title of best chip shop in Amsterdam in the annual French fries test of the Dutch daily *Algemeen Dagblad*.

29 PAR HASARD

Ceintuur-
baan 113-115
De Pijp ③
+31 (0)20 471 40 52
www.cafeparhasard.nl

More of a restaurant than a chip shop, Par Hasard is clearly inspired by its French and Belgian counterparts. They serve chips and snacks, as well as meals which you can wash down with a glass of beer or wine. It is consistently awarded a high score in a national newspaper's annual best chip test. They opened a second location in Amsterdam West, at 22, Douwes Dekkerstraat.

30 FRIETBOUTIQUE

Johannes
Verhulststraat 107
Museum Q ③
+31 (0)20 664 08 09
www.frietboutique.nl

The IJsboutique sells ice creams on sunny summer days. But what to do during the winter? The owners decided to start selling French fries and snacks. Successfully it seems, because the deep frying pan now runs all year round.

The 5 best places to eat
BITTERBALLEN

---

31 DE BALLENBAR
AT: FOOD HALLEN
Hannie Dankbaar
Passage 33
West ④
www.deballenbar.com

The Hallen is a covered market with food stands, a library, galleries, shops and a cinema. It opened in 2014 in a former tram depot. Due to the hype, it can get quite busy making it hard to find a table. One of the reasons to go there are De Ballenbar's *bitterballen*. Their bouillabaisse ball with brown shrimp inside is a treat and was invented by Michelin-starred chef Peter Gast.

32 HOFTUIN
Nieuwe Heren-
gracht 18-A
Plantage Q ②
+31 (0)20 370 27 23
www.eatwelldogood.nl

Be surprised by the bar snacks at Hoftuin, an 'all-day brunch restaurant' in a somewhat hidden garden next to the Hermitage Museum, which is surrounded by monumental buildings. Everything on the menu is homemade using only fresh and organic ingredients.

33 CAFÉ LUXEMBOURG
Spui 24
Old Centre ②
+31 (0)20 620 62 64
www.luxembourg.nl

Their veal *bitterbal* is the very best in town, according to a food critic whose job it was to test the products of 140 Amsterdam cafes. The *bitterballen* on Luxembourg's menu are made by the Amsterdam pastry shop Holtkamp. They also serve Holtkamp's shrimp *bitterballen*.

34 CAFÉ STEVENS

Geldersekade 123
Old Centre ②
+31 (0)20 620 69 70

There's only one place to enjoy a real *bitterbal*. In a real Amsterdam bar, of course. Café Stevens is one of those typical watering holes, to which locals flock in the morning to enjoy a coffee and read the newspaper. After work, people pop in for a beer and after a few rounds decide they can't resist the lure of the tasty *bitterbal*.

35 CAFÉ-RESTAURANT AMSTERDAM

Watertorenplein 6
Westerpark Q ④
+31 (0)20 682 26 66
www.caferestaurant amsterdam.nl

Café Restaurant Amsterdam is housed in a former pumping station of the municipal water company. It was built around 1900. From the inside, the cafe is spacious, bright and has an industrial vibe. It serves Oma Bobs *bitterballen* and Holtkamp shrimp croquettes, both from Amsterdam, as well as a mid-priced lunch and dinner menu, and a nice selection of beers.

The 5 best places for a
TASTY BURGER

---

36 THE BUTCHER

Albert Cuypstraat 129
De Pijp ③
+31 (0)20 470 78 75
www.the-butcher.com

The Butcher is a good spot to start out your evening in De Pijp, stocking up on food before exploring the numerous bars, or to end a day of shopping. The Butcher is known for its fresh, tasty burgers and crispy Belgian fries, but it has a secret. Behind the fridge door is a speak-easy with cocktails galore. On invitation only.

37 THRILL GRILL

Gerard Doustraat 98
De Pijp ③
+31 (0)20 760 67 50
www.thrillgrill.nl

This restaurant is the brainchild of TV chef Robert Kranenborg, who wanted to create the perfect burger. The result is called 'The classic beef thriller', with Brandt and Levie bacon, and a trademarked classic thriller sauce. Also on the menu: hotdogs and Caesar salads. Second location at 1e Constantijn Huygensstraat 35.

38 SMOKIN' BARRELS

Beukenplein 22
Oosterpark Q ⑤
+31 (0)20 693 35 55
www.smokinbarrels.nl

Lobsters and burgers cooked on smoking barrels (charcoal barbecues), served with craft beer and gin and tonics. It's a bustling place in the eastern part of town with a big, fenced off terrace with heaters in winter. On the weekend, they do a good brunch, with eggs Benedict and blueberry pancakes.

39 THE DUTCH WEED BURGER JOINT

Nicolaas Beets-
straat 47
West ④
+31 (0)20 331 29 30
*www.dutchweed
burger.com*

These healthy and tasty Dutch Weed Burgers used to be a foodtruck-exclusive, but the inventors recently opened their own 'joint' near the Foodhallen, claiming to be the world's first vegan-seaweed-fastfood-bar. The patties are made of soy and Royal Kumbu winter seaweed, which is harvested in National Park Oosterschelde. The buns and Weed Sauce also contain algae and seaweed.

40 BURGER 'N SHAKE

Land van
Cocagneplein 1-D
Watergraafsmeer ⑤
+31 (0)20 221 28 56
*www.burgers
enshakes.nl*

Here you can buy a burger for the price of a McDonald's burger, but that's where the similarities end. Burger 'n Shake only uses fresh, halal meat from animals that graze freely. Fries and veggies are freshly cut, milkshakes are made from organic milk.

37 THRILL GRILL

The 5 best places to eat
FRESH FISH

---

41 MOSSEL & GIN

Gosschalklaan 12
Westerpark Q ④
+31 (0)20 486 58 69
www.mosselengin.nl

Mossel & Gin specialises in, well, mussels, gin and tonic. When it opened, the owners wanted to upgrade the mussel's image and add something else to the typical steaming black pot. Also on the menu are oysters from Zeeland, lobster, crab and shrimp croquettes. Mossel & Gin is located in Westerpark and has a nice patio.

42 VIS AAN DE SCHELDE

Scheldeplein 4
South ⑥
+31 (0)20 675 15 83
www.visaandeschelde.nl

Vis aan de Schelde is one of the best fish restaurants in town. The menu changes every ten weeks, and consists of fresh seasonal fish. Lunch is available on weekdays from noon to 3.30 pm, dinner is served every day from 6.30 to 11 pm. Make sure to book ahead.

43 KRAS HARING

Kattenburgerplein
(in front of Scheep-
vaartmuseum)
Oostelijke Eilanden ②
+31 (0)299 36 84 30

It's a Dutch tradition: *haringhappen*. Grab the herring by its tail, dip it in raw onions if you like, and chow down. Kras Haring, an outdoor fish stall, is an excellent place to have one.

44 THE SEAFOOD BAR

Van Baerlestraat 5
Museum Q ③
+31 (0)20 670 83 55
www.theseafoodbar.nl

Various kinds of oysters, fish and chips, lobster or sushi: name something fishy and The Seafood Bar has it. All the fish is fresh and very tasty and, where possible, organic. The bar has an industrial design, and an open kitchen in the back. There's a second branch at Spui 15 and one at Ferdinand Bolstraat 32 in De Pijp.

45 BRIDGES

Oudezijds
Voorburgwal 197
Old Centre ②
+31 (0)20 555 35 60
*www.bridges
restaurant.nl*

Chef Joris Bijdendijk earned his first Michelin star at Bridges. This chic fish restaurant belongs to The Grand hotel. The building itself, however, used to have a slightly more down to earth purpose: it was the city council's canteen. Bridges participates in an organisation called Slow Food, which promotes the use of 'endangered' ingredients, like specific types of rye and spices.

41 MOSSEL EN GIN

The 5 best places to have a
GOOD PIZZA

46 PINSA'S

Spaarndammer-
straat 772
Westerpark Q ④
+31 (0)20 386 86 80
pinsas.nl

Pinsa's was named best national pizzeria several times. The cooks let the dough rise for 72 hours, and prepare all the pizzas and toppings on the spot. Your pizza might take longer to get at your table than at your regular pizzeria as a result. Order online and choose 'eat in our restaurant' if you really don't like waiting.

47 PAZZI

Eerste Looiers-
dwarsstraat 4
De Jordaan ①
+31 (0)20 320 28 00
www.pazzi
amsterdam.nl

Pazzi started with a tiny restaurant and take-away at the edge of the Jordaan. Their pizzas gained popularity quite quickly, so they opened a new and bigger restaurant in Declercqstraat. Try their Pikante, a spicy pizza with smoked Sicilian cheese, or the Tartufo with Parma ham and truffle sauce.

48 YAM YAM

Frederik Hendrik-
straat 88-90
West ④
+31 (0)20 681 50 97
www.yamyam.nl

Yam Yam is one of those pizza places that always seems to be full, no matter what time of evening. They don't only sell pizzas, but pastas as well, and they serve a classic *torta al limone* (lemon pie) for dessert.

49 IL PECORINO

Van der Pekplein 11
North ⑦
+31 (0)20 737 15 11
www.ilpecorino.nl

Il Pecorino is located on the north banks of the River IJ until fall 2016, so enjoy their nice terrace with spectacular views while it lasts. The classic Margherita DOC is simply to die for, but you can also try a *pizza bianca* (without tomato sauce) or a *calzone*. They have Florentine specialty beers to accompany your pizza, as well as a good selection of wines.

50 SOTTO LEGALE

Roelof Hartstraat 27
Museum Q ③
+31 (0)20 774 06 70
www.sottopizza.nl

As in all good pizza places, the wood oven takes centre stage here. Sitting in the front of the restaurant, you can watch the pizzas being shoved into the oven. If you sit on the mezzanine, you can practically feel the oven's heat rising up through your seat. They make real Neapolitan pizzas here. Try the *carnevales*, they have ricotta hidden in the crust. Yum!

The 5 best places to
DINE ON THE WATER

---

51 VUURTOREN EILAND

Oostelijke
Handelskade 34
EMBARK: VEEMKADE,
OPPOSITE LLOYD HOTEL
Oostelijke Eilanden ②
+31 (0)6 155 83 838
www.vuurtoreneiland.nl

Dining in a nature reserve on Vuurtoren-eiland became an instant hit when it was launched in 2013. You reach the island by boat and have dinner in a glass greenhouse while watching the sun set. The first restaurant burnt down, but now they're back, bigger and stronger, with a summer and winter restaurant, and plans so guests can stay the night. Reserve well ahead.

52 LOKAAL EDEL

Postjesweg 1
West ④
+31 (0)20 799 50 00
www.lokaaledel.nl

The waterside patio of this bar-restaurant is one of the most scenic locations in the Baarsjes district. This monumental building from the 1920s was built in Amsterdamse School style. The menu changes every three months, offering an affordable selection of lunch and dinner options. Edel organises popular afternoon drinks on every last Friday of the month.

53 PONT 13

Haparandadam 50
West ④
+31 (0)20 770 27 22
www.pont13.nl

A 1920s ferryboat converted into a restaurant outside of the city centre in a quiet harbour area with nice views. The old, authentic setting makes for a romantic night out. It's also a popular wedding venue. Especially when sunny, it's best to book ahead, to avoid being disappointed after a long trip.

54 REM-EILAND

Haparandadam 45-2
Westerpark Q ④
+31 (0)20 688 55 01
www.remeiland.com

REM-Eiland is an artificial island that was built in the 1960s in the North Sea to broadcast (illegal) commercial TV programmes. The pirate island was used for less than a year, but was later converted into a governmental measuring station. The island was eventually demolished and reassembled in Amsterdam's harbour in 2006. It offers spectacular views and some fine dining as well.

55 GS BRUNCH BOAT

Prinsengracht
263-267
PICK UP/DROP OFF:
HOMOMONUMENT –
KEIZERSGRACHT 198
De Jordaan ①
*www.reallynice
place.com*

If you're looking for a real treat, consider embarking on Gs brunch boat. Every Saturday and Sunday, it leaves from Westermarkt for a tour of the canals. Meanwhile, you get to choose from delicious cocktails (a mimosa or a bloody Mary), scrumptious steak and eggs or French toast, and finish it off with coffee and a brownie. The best way to start your weekend!

The 5 best places to eat
ASIAN FOOD

---

56 FOU FOW RAMEN
Elandsgracht 2-A
De Jordaan ①
+31 (0)20 845 05 44
www.foufow.nl

There's really nothing more comforting than a big bowl of steaming noodle soup. Fou Fow Ramen is a basic restaurant with a simple menu. Choose from four types of broth, and add your preferred toppings. Have a Japanese beer or a small cup of sake with your soup.

57 KHAN
Nederhoven 9
South ⑥
+31 (0)20 646 37 22

Don't be distracted by Khan's functional interior, because its courses are tasty and packed with flavour. Try the bacon and squid bulgogi or kimchi pancakes. You'll find a tiny Koreatown in Buitenveldert, with a handful of Korean restaurants. Take Metro 51 to Westwijk and get off at Van Boshuizenstraat.

58 PHO 91
Albert Cuypstraat 91
De Pijp ③
+31 (0)20 752 68 80
www.pho91.nl

Vietnamese street food in a small and cosy restaurant in De Pijp. *Pho* is a noodle soup that's originally from North Vietnam where it's primarily eaten at breakfast. But at Pho 91 you can eat four different kinds of *pho* (one veggie option) for dinner. It's only open for lunch in the weekend.

59 NAM KEE

Zeedijk 111-113
Old Centre ②
+31 (0)20 624 34 70
www.namkee.nl

This classic Cantonese restaurant opened in 1981 at Zeedijk, in the heart of the Chinese district. It acquired national fame as the setting for the book and film *Oysters at Nam Kee*, named after their popular steamed oyster dish. As it's also very popular with the members of the Chinese community, they opened two more locations at Nieuwmarkt and Marie Heinekenplein.

60 SONGKRAN

Marnixstraat 86
De Jordaan ①
+31 (0)20 320 45 62
www.songkran.nl

This Thai restaurant is tucked away along a main street, but is within walking distance of The Jordaan. Locals know that this is the place to go for the best red curries and *tom kha kai* (spicy chicken soup). The restaurant itself is simply, but tastefully decorated. The dishes are refined and made fresh, and the host is very friendly.

The 5 nicest places to go for
BREAKFAST

---

61 **COFFEE AND COCONUTS**

Ceintuurbaan
282-284
De Pijp ③
+31 (0)20 354 11 04
www.ctamsterdam.nl

This magnificent building with high ceilings and split levels was a cinema built in the 1920s. It was recently renovated and is now a zen blend of light wooden furniture, bare brick walls and the occasional plant, that seems to attract hipsters and mothers with babies alike. It's a perfect spot for lounging, chatting or working. They serve breakfast until 1 pm.

62 **LIBERTINE COMPTOIR DE CUISINE**

Berenstraat 20
Negen Straatjes ①
+31 (0)6 215 78 020
+31 (0)20 308 43 10
www.libertine.
amsterdam

This cafe is the little sister of Cafe Libertine in nearby Wolvenstraat, and only serves French toast (gluten-free options available). Have it for breakfast, lunch or dinner, with sweet toppings like vanilla and pecan or with a savoury twist? We dare you to try the French toast with lobster or eggs benedict!

63 **GREENWOODS**

Singel 103
Old Centre ②
+31 (0)20 623 70 71
www.greenwoods.eu

Sitting in Greenwoods is like taking part in a big, cosy British tea party. The location on Singel is quite small. If you do manage to grab a seat, try the eggs royale (poached with salmon on English muffins). Breakfast is served all day. In the afternoons, they do high teas as well.

64 STEK

Wibautstraat 95-97
Oosterpark Q ⑤
+31 (0)6 365 77 000
www.stek-
amsterdam.com

Wibautstraat is basically a long, straight racing track with a distinct communist feel, like the Allees you find in Berlin, but things are changing. New hotels, stylish clubs and laidback restaurants are popping up everywhere. Stek opens at 8 am (10 am on the weekend) and serves yoghurt and fruits, eggs Benedict or a full English breakfast, accompanied by excellent coffee.

65 KESSENS

Rozengracht 24
De Jordaan ①
+31 (0)20 221 74 31
www.kessens
amsterdam.nl

Sit down and enjoy a full breakfast with a glass of Prosecco. The owners believe that life is meant to be enjoyed. Anna used to work in Sweden, which is visible in Kessens' crisp and clean interior. Casper is a descendant of the famous Holtkamp patisserie family. Of course they serve some Holtkamp classics like shrimp croquettes and veal *bitterballen*.

65 KESSENS

The 5 most **CLASSY** but
CASUAL RESTAURANTS

---

66 **SCHEEPSKAMEEL**

Kattenburgerstraat 7,
building 24
Oostelijke Eilanden ②
+31 (0)20 337 96 80
www.scheepskameel.nl

This elegant but affordable restaurant opened in summer 2016 in the former naval area to the east of the city centre that will be completely revitalised. The menu features several dishes – you choose a raw dish, a vegetable dish and a meat or fish dish followed by dessert. Watch the chefs as they carefully prepare your food in the extremely open kitchen.

67 **CAFÉ MODERN**

Meidoornweg 2
North ⑦
+31 (0)20 494 06 84
*www.modern
amsterdam.nl*

Subtly balanced, rich flavours... that is what you get at Café Modern. Like sweetbread with chorizo, or a Jerusalem artichoke soup. The fixed five-course menu changes weekly though. This restaurant is located in an old bank building, therefore the acoustics can be challenging. Spot the old safe in the basement. Upstairs, you can stay the night in boutique hotel Sweet Dreamz.

67 CAFE MODERN

68 TOSCANINI

Lindengracht 75
De Jordaan ①
+31 (0)20 623 28 13
www.restaurant
toscanini.nl

A classic when it comes to Italian restaurants. Toscanini has a fanatical fan base in Amsterdam. Some customers have been coming here for decades and are handing down this tradition to the next generations. It's a friendly neighbourhood restaurant where you can sit down for hours, eat six courses of Italian slow food, drink three bottles of wine, and, after that last glass of grappa, find out that it's already way past your bedtime.

69 BAR ALT

Stadionplein 103
South ⑥
+31 (0)6 30 94 18 99
www.bar-alt.com

Of course you can have wine with your food, but why not be a little more adventurous for once? When it comes to pairing great food with great craft beer, Bar Alt stands out in a crowd of competitors. In summer, Bar Alt has a large terrace out front. In winter head inside to enjoy the stylish industrial interior.

70 GUTS & GLORY

Utrechtsestraat 6
Canal Belt South ③
+31 (0)20 362 00 30
www.gutsglory.nl

Best friends Guillaume de Beer and Freek van Noortwijk used to cook at Daalder in De Jordaan. They are only in their mid-twenties, but opened this restaurant in early 2015. They didn't want to be 'just another chicken restaurant', so every six months, they put another animal centre stage. And with boyish bravura, they intend to use every part of that animal. Also open for lunch.

The 5 best places to enjoy a
HEALTHY LUNCH

---

71 **GARTINE**
Taksteeg 7
Old Centre ②
+31 (0)20 320 41 32
www.gartine.nl

Tucked away in an alley between the busy Kalverstraat and Rokin, Gartine serves delicious breakfast and lunch in their cosy restaurant. They grow fruit and veg in their own cottage garden outside Amsterdam. Their selection of pies is mouth-watering, with surprising combinations and strong flavours, changing with the seasons.

72 **INSTOCK**
Czaar Peterstraat 21
Oostelijke Eilanden ②
+31 (0)20 363 57 65
www.instock.nl

Every morning, the Instock 'food rescue team' visits nearby supermarkets to collect food that is close to its expiration date. They use these products which would otherwise be thrown away to prepare tasty dishes and meals. Brown bananas are turned into banana ice-cream, old bread into French toast or grilled cheese. Can you think of a more creative way to fight food waste?

73 VENKEL

Albert Cuypstraat 22
De Pijp ③
+31 (0)20 772 31 98
www.venkelsalades.nl

Old-fashioned wooden crates are filled with vegetables that all seem to have won a beauty contest. At Venkel local products are turned into salads on demand, and hearty soups. Try their rhubarb lemonade or a fresh ginger tea to wash down the organic veggies.

74 STADSKANTINE

Van Woustraat 120
De Pijp ③
+31 (0)20 774 18 47
www.destadskantine.nl

The Stadkantine is a prime spot for Macbook toting hipsters and students writing their term papers, mostly because of the Wi-Fi and cheap, but very decent and healthy food. Order at the counter where food is immediately dished up on your plate. The Stadskantine is open for breakfast, lunch and dinner, but unlike a real canteen, this is actually a nice place to sit down and enjoy some good people-watching or have a conversation.

75 LAVINIA GOOD FOOD

Kerkstraat 176
Canal Belt South ③
+31 (0)20 626 14 32
*www.lavinia
goodfood.nl*

Lavinia serves three types of veggie cocktails (green, orange and red), and big sourdough sandwiches for lunch, with mashed avocado, tuna or grilled pepper, or spelt pizzettas with lamb or salmon. If you're lucky, there might be a space on the comfy leather sofa. A second location opened at Amstelveenseweg 192.

75 LAVINIA GOOD FOOD

CAFÉ SCHILLER

70 PLACES FOR A DRINK

The 5 best
BREWERS
in Amsterdam

---

76 **BROUWERIJ 'T IJ**
Funenkade 7
Indische buurt ⑤
+31 (0)20 261 98 01
www.brouwerijhetij.nl

The pulse of beer-crazy Amsterdammers quickens at the thought of this old mill. Brouwerij 't IJ long predates the current beer craze, when some brewers started to semi-illegally brew their own beers in the eighties. The brewery and tasting room are located in a former bathhouse and there's a large patio outside.

77 **DE PRAEL**
Oudezijds
Armsteeg 26
Old Centre ②
+31 (0)20 408 44 69
www.deprael.nl

De Prael isn't just a brewery with a nice bar, it's also a social enterprise that employs people suffering from mental illness. Arno Kooy and Fer Kok were hobby brewers working in mental health care when they founded De Prael. Instead of applying for grants, they invest everything they earn.

78 **OEDIPUS**
Gedempt Hamer-
kanaal 85
North ⑦
www.oedipus
brewing.com

Four friends started brewing beer in their attics and are now taking Amsterdam's bars by storm. They're known for their exciting flavours. Try their Mannenliefde, a 'saison' with lemongrass and spicy peppercorns, or Mama, pale ale with Motueka hops.

79 **BROUWERIJ KLEIBURG**

AT: DE PROEFZAAK
Hullenbergweg 6
Southeast
+31 (0)20 210 17 03
www.brouwerij
kleiburg.nl

Kleiburg used to be a notorious Bijlmer apartment building and was almost demolished. Fortunately it was saved and the apartments were renovated, among others by a Christian community. They founded a convent and started to brew their own brand of beer as well. Try the Bijlmer's only beer in De Proefzaak (closed on Sundays).

80 **BUTCHER'S TEARS**

Karperweg 45
South ⑥
+31 (0)6 539 09 777
www.butchers-tears.com

Butcher's Tears has been brewing its fine beers since 2012, opening this canteen-like proeflokaal one year later. This place is one of a kind: the setting is very pleasant. On some nights they organise concerts and lectures. But the most important thing are their amazing beers. Such as Lipreader, a fruity and smoky winter ale, or Green Cap, an original Amsterdam pale ale brewed with hops from Eastern Europe.

80 BUTCHER'S TEARS

The 5 most traditional
CAFES IN DE JORDAAN

---

81 CAFÉ DE TUIN
**Tweede Tuin-
dwarsstraat 13**
De Jordaan ①
+31 (0)20 624 45 59
www.cafedetuin.nl

The Jordaan was the first gentrified working-class area of Amsterdam. In the mid nineties, it attracted many young professionals. Café De Tuin is a classic and down to earth bar, crammed with young Amsterdammers on weekends. De Tuin also serves sandwiches and snacks.

82 'T MONUMENTJE
Westerstraat 120
De Jordaan ①
+31 (0)20 624 35 41
www.monumentje.nl

't Monumentje is a small traditional pub where you'll find a group of regulars drinking, chatting and reading newspapers from morning until midnight. The coffee is really good and cheap at the same time. Regulars visit in October to join the backgammon tournament. The wall of fame is near the door.

83 CAFÉ LOWIETJE
**Derde Goudsbloem-
dwarsstraat 2**
De Jordaan ①
+31(0)20 427 81 98
www.cafelowietje.nl

There was always one certainty in every episode of the classic Dutch crime series Baantjer: at some point during the episode the main characters would go to Café Lowietje. It was there that detective De Cock and his side-kick Vledder would always have a break-through in their investigation.

84 DE KAT IN DE WIJNGAERT

Lindengracht 160
De Jordaan ①
+31 (0)20 622 45 54
www.dekatinde
wijngaert.nl

The Jordaan exploded in July 1886 when the authorities put a stop to the popular tradition of eel-heading, which involved stringing a live eel to a rope and pulling its head off. Twenty-six people died during the ensuing uproar. The so-called *Palingoproer* (eel revolt) started in front of De Kat in de Wijngaert (when Lindengracht was still a canal).

85 CAFÉ 'T SMALLE

Egelantiersgracht 12
De Jordaan ①
+31 (0)20 623 96 17
www.t-smalle.nl

Here, Pieter Hoppe opened his now famous Hoppe jenever distillery in 1780. Afterwards he moved to the city of Schiedam because he needed more space to make his popular spirit. The building now houses Café 't Smalle, which opened in 1978. The owners used an old painting showing the original interior design to reconstruct the bar's authentic look and feel.

84 DE KAT IN DE WIJNGAERT

The 5 best

COCKTAIL BARS

---

86 **VESPER BAR**
Vinkenstraat 57
De Jordaan ①
+31 (0)20 846 44 58
www.vesperbar.nl

This tiny cocktail bar just off Haarlemmer-dijk is an ode to Vesper Lynd, the 'only woman James Bond ever loved'. Bond is also present in the decoration of this elegant venue where you could easily spend the entire night. All the cocktails on the menu are listed in a matrix: strong, light, sour and sweet.

87 **HIDING IN PLAIN SIGHT**
Rapenburg 18
Old Centre ②
+31 (0)6 252 93 620
www.hps amsterdam.com

Chesterfield sofas, chandeliers and vintage photos: this tiny cocktail bar exudes a retro, roaring twenties atmosphere. Hiding in Plain Sight is easy-going and adds a humorous touch to the presentation of their fine mixes. Reservations are recommended.

88 **SKYLOUNGE DOUBLETREE HILTON**
Oosterdoksstraat 4
Old Centre ②
+31 (0)20 530 08 75
www.skylounge amsterdam.com

This restaurant and cocktail bar on the 11th floor of the DoubleTree Hilton has large windows and a rooftop terrace that offers panoramic views of the city. Prices at the SkyLounge are as high as the building in which it is located, but the view on the River IJ waterfront and the city centre is unrivalled.

89 DOOR74

**Reguliers-
dwarsstraat 74-I**
Canal Belt South ③
+31 (0)6 340 45 122
www.door-74.com

We 'strongly recommend' reserving ahead for Timo Janse-de Vries's exclusive cocktail bar Door74. The bar looks like a 1930s speakeasy, decorated with dark wood and antique barware. The menu changes four times a year, and they serve a daily special cocktail. Or just tell them what you like and they will mix you something special. Door74 was voted the 15th best bar in the world in 2013.

90 BAR OLDENHOF

Elandsgracht 84
De Jordaan ①
+31 (0)20 751 32 73
www.bar-oldenhof.com

What is it about cocktails? Why do they taste better in a classy, old-fashioned setting? Oldenhof has the darkest of interiors, organises whisky tastings, mixes great cocktails and plays some smooth jazz. So find a seat at the bar or in one of the comfy chairs and enjoy.

86 VESPER BAR

The 5 best places to have a good
CUP OF COFFEE

---

91 WHITE LABEL COFFEE

Jan Evertsenstraat 136
West ④
+31(0)20 737 13 59
www.whitelabelcoffee.nl

Francesco and Elmer opened their coffee roastery and bar in early 2014, after meeting in the Espressofabriek in Westerpark. It's the perfect hangout for a tremendous flat white or you can also just sit and read at their reading table. Their homeroasted beans are for sale, as are the artisanal chocolate bars from Amsterdam-based shop Chocolátl.

92 RUM BABA

Pretoriusstraat 33
Oosterpark Q ⑤
+31 (0)20 846 94 98
www.rumbaba.nl

This bright and airy corner shop is a veritable spot of sunshine in the eastern part of Amsterdam. It's the sister of nearby Cafe Bru and serves loose leaf tea imported straight from China as well as freshly-roasted coffee. Peckish? Their bakery serves American classics such as mud pie and lemon drizzle cake.

93 DE KOFFIESALON

1e Constantijn
Huygensstraat 82
West ④
+31 (0)20 612 40 79
www.dekoffiesalon.nl

This place serves Italian-style coffee in a cosy interior with beautiful stained glass windows. It is a lovely place to start your day with a cappuccino. If you're lucky, you can catch a few rays of sun on their tiny terrace.

94 **THE COFFEE VIRUS**
Overhoeksplein 2
North ⑦
+31 (0)6 537 29 978
www.thecoffeevirus.nl

The Coffee Virus is located in the former Shell laboratories, but it's definitely not your average cafeteria. This coffee hotspot is located in the lobby of A Lab, a work space where new media and technology start-ups and professionals meet. The Coffee Virus serves coffee from local roasters, as well as fresh salads, sandwiches and cakes.

95 **SCANDINAVIAN EMBASSY**
Sarphatipark 34
De Pijp ③
+31 (0)6 816 00 140
www.scandinavian embassy.nl

The blonde wood and white walls of the Scandinavian Embassy, on the fringe of Sarphati Park, make for a minimalistic but warm coffee bar. The owner is the award-winning Argentinean-born roaster Nicolas Castagno. After moving to Sweden in his twenties, he became involved in the Swedish coffee scene. He relocated to Amsterdam, where he started his own spot with a Scandinavian flavour.

The 5 cutest
BAR CATS

---

96 PRIKKIEDIK
@ CAFÉ PRIK
Spuistraat 109
Old Centre ②
+31 (0)20 320 00 02
www.prikamsterdam.nl

Café PRIK is a popular gay bar with a familiar and open setting. Their bar cat Prikkiedik (a pun on the name of the ginger cartoon cat Dikkie Dik) is as old as the bar. If you want to make her happy, just put a bowl of water on the rocks (or is it vodka?) on the bar.

97 CLAUS @ CAFÉ BAX
Ten Katestraat 119
West ④
+31 (0)20 612 23 43
www.cafebax.nl

Claus just happened to walk in on the day his predecessor Trix (named after our former Queen) was run over. His previous owner, a butcher, did try to reclaim him, but Claus preferred to stay at this livingroom cafe. He's a very friendly ginger tomcat, and doesn't mind being petted, even when he's sleeping.

98 FENDER @ CAFÉ
SOUND GARDEN
Marnixstraat 164-166
De Jordaan ①
+31 (0)20 620 28 53
*www.cafesound
garden.nl*

'Casa di Fender', says this bar cat's favourite box. She used to have a little sister called Gibson, who disappeared after an adventure, while Fender walked straight into the next-door police station and was safely returned. Fender likes to scratch boxes and eat from the bartenders' hands.

99 MAUP @ BLAAUWHOOFT

Hendrik Jonker-plein 1
Westelijke Eilanden ①
+31 (0)20 623 87 21
www.blaauwhooft.nl

Maurits (Maup) Caransa was an Amsterdam real estate tycoon who was kidnapped in 1977. It is quite likely that the Rote Armee Fraction was behind it. Café Blaauwhooft's cat Maup is named after Caransa. This slender black cat with its white bib ('tuxedo cat') likes to parade around this laidback cafe-restaurant as if it were his country estate.

100 FIDEL @ CAFÉ DE WETERING

Weteringstraat 37
Canal Belt South ③
+31 (0)20 622 96 76

This ginger and white tomcat likes to roam around. He's been known to fall into a canal once or twice, and was even stuck in someone's garden once. But he keeps on coming back to Café de Wetering, where he has his own house-shaped box on the window sill.

99 MAUP @ BLAAUWHOOFT

The 5 bars with the
LONGEST BEER MENU

---

101 CAFÉ GOLLEM

Raamsteeg 4
Old Centre ②
+31 (0)20 612 94 44
www.cafegollem.nl

Café Gollem is a tiny brown cafe, located in a former distillery in an alley off Spuistraat. It was the very first speciality beer bar in Amsterdam when it opened in 1974. Gollem serves 14 draft beers and about 200 bottled beers. It now has four branches.

102 IN DE WILDEMAN

Kolksteeg 3
Old Centre ②
+31 (0)20 638 23 48
www.indewildeman.nl

At one time the premises of Café In de Wildeman were used by the distillery Levert & Co. and still have a very authentic look and feel. Wooden barrels, old billboards and beer paraphernalia decorate the walls. But the beer list is what really makes the difference: 18 different draft beers and 250 bottled beers, mainly from Belgium and the Netherlands.

103 ARENDSNEST

Herengracht 90
Haarlemmer Q ①
+31 (0)20 421 20 57
www.arendsnest.nl

Arendsnest is one of a kind because it's the only specialised beer cafe in Amsterdam that only serves Dutch beer. That doesn't mean they don't have a large selection. You can choose from 30 draft beers and 100 bottled beers. Tastings are offered in the basement.

104 WESTERDOK

Westerdoksdijk 715-A
Westelijke Eilanden ①
+31 (0)20 428 96 70
www.cafewesterdok.nl

Steve Bramwell and Adelina Landman run Café Westerdok, a historic bar that was established in 1899. Westerdok is a so-called free house, meaning that it has no ties to any brewery. The owners can therefore only serve the beers they like. The smoking area is especially unique: a 55-square metre basement with billiard tables, dartboards and lounge chairs.

105 CRAFT & DRAFT

Overtoom 417
West ④
+31 (0)20 223 07 25
www.craftanddraft.nl

Craft & Draft's interior is functional with minimalistic decorations and very few places to sit. But once inside, prepare yourself to take a journey around the world of beer. Contrary to the menus of many cafes, Craft & Draft serves about 140 beers from places like Scandinavia, England, Spain and the United States. The cafe has a small storefront, where you can buy beers to take home.

104 WESTERDOK

The 5 best places to

PARTY AFTER DARK

---

106 CLAIRE

Rembrandtplein 17
Old Centre ②
www.claire.nl

This club was formerly known as Studio 80 but reopened in late 2016 with a lighter and friendlier ambiance, renaming itself Claire. It's conveniently located near busy Rembrandtplein and is definitely the top option around here. You can dance till your pants drop. Claire closes at 8 am on the weekend.

107 WAREHOUSE ELEMENTENSTRAAT

Elementenstraat 25
New-West ④
+31 (0)900 660 66 06
www.elementen
straat.nl

The western dock area was the scene for many (illegal) rave parties in the nineties. The warehouse at Elementenstraat 25 was closed for years, but re-opened in spring 2014 as Warehouse Elementenstraat. The venue still has an industrial feel to it and hosts regular techno and house parties for up to 2500 revellers.

108 DE SCHOOL

Dr Jan van
Breemenstraat 1
New-West ④
+31 (0)20 737 31 97
*www.deschool
amsterdam.nl*

Located in a former technical school, De School hosts top DJs from around the world in their basement. There's also a concert venue, a gallery, a fabulous restaurant, a garden with terrace and a yoga and fitness school, so more than enough entertainment to fill the 24 hours in a day.

109 DE MARKTKANTINE

Jan van Galenstraat 6
West ④
+31 (0)20 732 17 60
www.marktkantine.nl

The former Marcanti building was built in the 1930s as a canteen for people working in the neighbouring market halls (which nowadays is called Food Center Amsterdam). It was subsequently converted into a theatre and a discotheque, but closed its doors in 2010. Four years later, it re-opened and now it hosts regular club evenings as well as having an American-style BBQ restaurant.

110 RADION

Louwesweg 1
New-West ④
+31 (0)20 452 47 09
*www.radion
amsterdam.nl*

This used to be a school where dentists trained but now it's home to one of the more innovative and original cultural platforms of Amsterdam. Located out west, Radion organises regular club nights, performances and lectures. Thanks to their 24-hour permit, nights seamlessly blend into days.

The 5 most pleasant
LIVING ROOM CAFES

---

111 KRITERION

Roetersstraat 170
Plantage Q ②
+31 (0)20 623 17 08
www.kriterion.nl

When the Nazis occupied Amsterdam in WWII, a group of resisting students helped about a thousand Jewish children to go into hiding. After the war, the students started a commercial movie theatre, allowing students to work and graduate without being financially dependent. The cinema and cafe are still very popular with students.

112 DE RUYSCHKAMER

Ruyschstraat 34-H
Oosterpark Q ⑤
+31 (0)20 670 36 22
www.deruyschkamer.nl

Everything in De Ruyschkamer is for sale. And not just the healthy juices, the peanut butter sandwiches, the excellent *bitterballen* and specialty beers. The retro furniture and vintage curiosities can also be bought.

113 CAFÉ L'AFFICHE

Jacob van Lennep-
straat 39-HS
West ④
+31 (0)20 612 19 59
www.cafelaffiche.nl

Locals and tourists meet here, drawn in by the cosy interior, the friendly staff, and walls full of old and new posters (hence the name). Their cheese toasties are unrivalled and available well into the night. But the biggest draw might be the huge west-facing terrace, with plenty of late afternoon sunshine!

114 CAFÉ BRECHT

Weteringschans 157
Canal Belt South ③
+31 (0)20 627 22 11
www.cafebrecht.nl

At Café Brecht, it feels as if someone has turned back time. Tacky lampshades, colourful floral wallpaper, and old but very comfortable furniture. Brecht is an oldschool, German-style and 'gemütlich' living room cafe with German beer on the menu.

115 BAR JOOST

Molukkenstraat 33
Indische Buurt ⑤
+31 (0)6 437 48 787
www.joost-
amsterdam.nl

Bar Joost opened its doors in 2014 in the up-and-coming Indische Buurt and soon became a neighbourhood favourite. They serve delicious locally roasted coffee, ciders, lemonades, whiskys, cocktails and forty beers sourced exclusively from Amsterdam brewers. Beware of the ship's bell above the bar, if you ring it you have to buy everyone a round.

114 CAFÉ BRECHT

The 5 most
STYLISH CAFES

―――――

116 CAFÉ SCHILLER

Rembrandtplein 24
Old Centre ②
+31 (0)20 624 98 46
www.cafeschiller.nl

Inside Café Schiller it seems as if time stopped in 1913. Originally it was just a hotel, the bar was added in the early 1920s. It soon became a hotspot for artists and sophisticated city dwellers. Frequent visitors included the sculptor Ossip Zadkine and the comedian Fien de la Mar. Numerous paintings from that era still decorate the building.

117 TUNES BAR – CONSERVATORIUM HOTEL

Van Baerlestraat 27
Museum Q ③
+31 (0)20 570 00 00
*www.conservatorium
hotel.com/restaurants-
and-bars/tunes-bar*

The Tunes Bar is a stylish cocktail bar in the Conservatorium Hotel. It has a vibrant metropolitan ambiance, even Madonna and Lady Gaga were spotted here. The building dates from 1901 and used to be the headquarters of the national savings bank, until the Amsterdam conservatory moved here in 1984. It was converted into a hotel in 2011, based on a design by Italian architect Piero Lissoni.

118 CAFÉ DE JAREN

**Nieuwe Doelen-
straat 20-22**
Old Centre ②
+31 (0)20 625 57 71
www.cafedejaren.nl

Rembrandt van Rhijn lived at 20-22, Nieuwe Doelenstraat for two years. But nowadays you'll find one of Amsterdam's larger grand cafes here. Café de Jaren spans two floors. The large windows and the patio with a view of the Amstel River are a great draw. Visitors with boats use the private dock for mooring.

119 GRAND CAFÉ-
RESTAURANT
1E KLAS

Stationsplein 15
**Central Station –
Platform 2B**
Old Centre ②
+31 (0)20 625 01 31
*www.restaurant
1eklas.nl*

Grand Café-Restaurant 1e Klas ('first class') has a grand, Art Nouveau feel to it and is located near platform 2B in Amsterdam Central Station. It's a popular place for short business meetings, interviews and appointments. The station, including 1e Klas, was built between 1882 and 1889 by the architect Pierre Cuypers, who also designed the Rijksmuseum.

120 CAFÉ AMERICAIN

Leidsekade 97
Canal Belt South ③
+31 (0)20 556 30 10
www.cafeamericain.nl

There is a story about the Dutch writer Harry Mulisch. In the early years of his career, he liked to visit Café Americain, an Amsterdam establishment that was built in 1902 in the art nouveau style that was so popular with artists and writers. Mulisch liked to have himself announced by an employee: 'Phone call for Mr. Mulisch!' As a result, many people already knew his name before becoming familiar with his work.

The 5 nicest places for a drink
ON THE WATERFRONT

---

121 HOTEL BUITEN
Th. J. Lammerslaan 3
West ④
+31 (0)20 331 79 00
www.hotelbuiten.nl

Located on the banks of Sloterplas, this terrace offers a great view of the lake and some sail boats if you're lucky. It's easy to while away an entire day here, going for a swim or playing some games in front of the fireplace on colder days. Sample some of their fresh juices and delicious snacks while you're at it.

122 HANNEKE'S BOOM
Dijksgracht 4
Oostelijke Eilanden ②
+31 (0)20 419 98 20
www.hannekesboom.nl

Hanneke's Boom was first featured on a city map in 1662. It was the entrance to one of the waterways leading into the city. Here the authorities checked everything that came in and went out of the city. In 2011, a popular bar opened here. The terrace is on the water level.

123 DE CEUVEL
Korte Papaverweg 4
North ⑦
+31 (0)20 229 62 10
www.cafedeceuvel.nl

The Amsterdam North city council held a competition to find a new use for an old, polluted shipyard. A group of young entrepreneurs came up with a plan to build an entirely self-supporting and sustainable cafe including a waterless urinal, soil-cleaning vegetation and solar panels on the roof.

124 DE WATERKANT

Marnixstraat 246
De Jordaan ①
+31 (0)20 737 11 26
www.waterkant
amsterdam.nl

Nobody could have imagined that the area below the Europarking garage would one day become a vibrant bar-restaurant. Well, it did. Waterkant refers to the boulevard along the Surinam river in Paramaribo, a popular meeting place for locals. The Amsterdam version can get quite crowded too. The bar offers a great selection of beers, bar food (nachos, chicken wings, salads), and dinner after 5.30 pm.

125 PLLEK

T.T. Neveritaweg 59
North ⑦
+31 (0)20 290 00 20
www.pllek.nl

Pllek is a bar and restaurant on the shore of 't IJ. On sunny days, the patio (or rather their spacious city beach) can get very crowded, at night campfires are lit. Pllek serves breakfast, lunch and dinner. Most dishes are organic using seasonal and regional products.

124 DE WATERKANT

The 5 best places to drink
SPIRITS

—————

126 WHISKYCAFÉ L&B

**Korte Leidse-
dwarsstraat 82-84
Canal Belt South ③
+31 (0)20 625 23 87
*www.whisky
proeverijen.nl***

The L&B Whisky cafe has a fantastic selection of over 1800 different types of whisky. The majority are Scottish, but the menu also features brands from Ireland, the United States and Japan. Don't worry if you don't know what to choose. The staff are very knowledgeable and they'll help you pick one you like.

127 WYNAND FOCKINK

**Pijlsteeg 31
Old Centre ②
+31 (0)20 639 26 95
*www.wynand-
fockink.nl***

The Wynand Fockink distillery opened in 1679. For centuries, it was a major distillery with branches in several European capitals. After WWII, its competitor Bols took over the distillery. Only the tasting room remained. Here you can still taste Wynand Fockink's homemade jenevers, brandies and old Dutch liqueurs such as 'drie maal drie', made of almonds, oranges and brandy.

128 'T NIEUWE DIEP

Flevopark 13
Indische Buurt ⑤
+31 (0)6 270 76 065
+31 (0)6 506 76 339
www.nwediep.nl

't Nieuwe Diep ('the new lake') is an artisan distillery and tasting room in the heart of Flevo Park. It opened in 2010 and has about 100 homemade jenevers, bitters and other drinks on offer; the majority are produced with organic ingredients. Cars are not allowed in the park, so you can only get here on foot or by bike.

129 DE DRIE FLESCHJES

Gravenstraat 18
Old Centre ②
+31 (0)20 624 84 43
www.dedriefleschjes.nl

This tasting room opened in 1650, during the era when jenever from distilleries in the northern Netherlands was sold all over the world. The floor is still covered in sand, which was considered hygienic at the time, and the counter is quite low, so you actually are forced to kneel when you want to take your first sip. It can be quite touristy.

130 PROEFLOKAAL DE OOIEVAAR

Sint Olofspoort 1
Old Centre ②
+31 (0)23 561 54 90
www.proeflokaal
deooievaar.nl

You wouldn't think so at first glance, but Zeedijk is actually a very mixed area. The many tourists draw the most attention, but Zeedijk also has several authentic Amsterdam bars where the locals come to enjoy a beer or a jenever. Tasting room De Ooievaar ('the stork') is one of them; it has a long list of jenevers and liqueurs.

The 5 nicest
COFFEESHOPS

---

131 KATSU
**Eerste v/d Helst-
straat 70**
De Pijp ③
www.katsu.nl

Described by one visitor as 'a coffeeshop for the cultured smoker', Katsu is a laidback shop where you can smoke weed while browsing the newspaper or talking to one of the regulars. In summertime, take a seat on the terrace out front, or head to Sarphati Park.

132 LA TERTULIA
Prinsengracht 312
De Jordaan ①
+31 (0)20 623 85 03

One of the friendliest coffeeshops in town. It looks like a cosy tearoom, with lots of plants inside and a nice seating area on the mezzanine, as well as a terrace overlooking the canal. On the painted store's brick front, look out for Vincent van Gogh, who's high on his art, or maybe it was weed…

133 SIBERIË
Brouwersgracht 11
Haarlemmer Q ①
+31 (0)20 623 59 09
*www.coffeeshop
siberie.nl*

This is one of those shops where you could take your mother to show her that there's really nothing wrong with coffeeshops. It's a clean, spacious and tidy shop in a quiet section of beautiful Brouwersgracht, but very close to Central Station. Siberië caters to tourists and locals alike.

134 **ABRAXAS**

Jonge Roelensteeg 12
Old Centre ②
+31 (0)20 625 57 63
www.abraxas.tv

Step into a psychedelic Alice in Wonderland scene, with swirling colours and flickering lights and maybe even a hookah-smoking caterpillar if you squint. Abraxas opened 25 years ago and is known for its central location, great atmosphere and friendly service.

135 **BOEREJONGENS**

Baarsjesweg 239
West ④
www.boerejongens.com

With its classy interior, Boerejongens feels like an old-fashioned apothecary. According to some, they sell the highest quality cannabis in town. The owner of the Boerejongens chain of coffeeshops (there are two more locations) also owns Amsterdam Genetics, a major seed supplier.

132 **LA TERTULIA**

The 5 places with the
NICEST TERRACES

---

136 **CAFÉ COOK**
James Cookstraat 2
West ④
+31 (0)20 612 05 47
www.cafecook.nl

Jan Maijenplein is a quiet square in Amsterdam West. It's just off the main street, with children playing soccer in front of the magnificent Jerusalem Church in the typical Amsterdamse School architectural style. Café Cook has a large terrace in one corner of the square. Have dinner or a drink here while enjoying the sun from the early afternoon onwards.

137 **DE LIEFDE**
Bilderdijkpark 1-A
West ④
+31 (0)20 389 23 54
www.deliefde
amsterdam.nl

The tiny Bilderdijkpark originally was a catholic cemetery during the 19th century. It had a small mortuary, designed by Jan David Zocher, who also created parts of Vondel Park. The mortuary was still there when the cemetery became a park. Wine bar De Liefde ('love', named after the cemetery) has a pleasant terrace, overlooking the small park.

138 CAFÉ-RESTAURANT DE PLANTAGE

Plantage Kerklaan 36
Plantage Q ②
+31 (0)20 760 68 00
www.caferestaurant
deplantage.nl

The former offices of Artis, Amsterdam's zoo, were recently converted into a state-of-the-art restaurant called De Plantage. The large wooden conservatory has space for 240 people with a spacious terrace facing the bird enclosure. So you might see some white spoonbills or flamingos while you dine.

139 VERGULDEN EENHOORN

Ringdijk 58
Watergraafsmeer ⑤
+31 (0)20 214 93 33
www.vergulden
eenhoorn.nl

The hustle and bustle of city life seems very far away when you enter this farm, which dates from 1702. There's a beautiful restaurant under the wooden beams of the former cowshed but the real draw is outside, namely the farm's fenced garden with magnolia trees, grassy lawns and flowers galore. A gorgeous place to spend a comfortable afternoon.

140 VONDELPARK3

Vondelpark
South ⑥
+31 (0)20 639 25 89
www.unlimitedlabel.
com/nl/vondelpark3

The Vondelpark Pavilion was built in the 1870s and used as an exhibition space. At one time the Filmmuseum was located here, until it moved to Amsterdam North in 2012. The pavilion was then completely renovated and reopened as VondelCS, a hotspot for media organisations. There's also a restaurant, Vondelpark3, which has two large terraces: one on the ground floor level, and one at the top of the staircase.

The 5 nicest places for
GAY AND LESBIANS

141 DE TRUT

Bilderdijkstraat 165-E
West ④
+31 (0)20 612 35 24
www.trutfonds.nl

In 1985, this squatted factory which had been converted into a discotheque became a gay club called De Trut ('the bitch'). It's been a liberal and artistic place since the eighties and is still going strong. The Sunday night parties are still very popular. The concept is simple: only gays, no cell phones and cheap drinks.

142 LELLEBEL

Utrechtsestraat 4
Canal Belt South ③
+31 (0)20 233 65 33
www.lellebel.nl

Transvestites run De Lellebel at the top of Utrechtsestraat. The bar's friendly staff invites everyone to talk to other guests or to join a playback show. You may feel shy upon entry, but you'll soon start to enjoy the easy-going atmosphere.

143 CAFÉ 'T MANDJE

Zeedijk 63
Old Centre ②
+31 (0)20 622 53 75
www.cafetmandje.nl

Bet van Beeren opened Café 't Mandje in 1927. Bet was a legendary character: she wore a leather coat and drove her motorcycle around town. She was openly gay, and her bar on Zeedijk was one of the first places where homosexuals and lesbians could openly meet. The Amsterdam Museum (at Kalverstraat 92) reconstructed parts of the cafe's old interior.

144 SAAREIN

Elandsstraat 119
De Jordaan ①
+31 (0)20 623 49 01
www.saarein2.nl

In 1978, a group of ten women joined forces and took over a pub in the Jordaan calling it Saarein. It became a place where lesbian women were able to enjoy themselves and each other without having to deal with the curious glances of macho men. Men were not admitted. But times have changed and nowadays, the bar is open to all 'queer-minded people'.

145 TABOO BAR

Reguliersdwars-
straat 45
Old Centre ②
+31 (0)20 775 39 63
www.taboobar.nl

The Reguliersdwarsstraat became Amsterdam's best-known gay street in the sixties, because it connected the gay scenes of Kerkstraat and a large discotheque in het Singel. Taboo Bar is a small and intimate gay bar with a good selection of cocktails.

142 LELLEBEL

MOOOI

80 PLACES
TO SHOP

5

WELL-STOCKED BOOKSTORES

146 HET MARTYRIUM

Van Baerlestraat 170-172
Museum Q ③
+31 (0)20 673 20 92
www.hetmartyrium.nl

There's a hushed library atmosphere in this bookshop. It's easy to spend an hour leafing through the books here. There's a particularly big sales section that offers a surprising range of old and new good books. The English literature, poetry and non-fiction sections are quite good as well.

147 ATHENAEUM

Spui 14-16
Old Centre ②
+31 (0)20 514 14 60
www.athenaeum.nl

Athenaeum, opened in the sixties, is well known for its large section of non-fiction and academic literature and has become the preferred supplier of cultural and academic institutions. The Nieuwscentrum next door probably has the best selection of foreign newspapers and magazines in town.

148 SCHELTEMA

Rokin 9
Old Centre ②
+31 (0)20 523 14 11
www.scheltema.nl

Scheltema was founded in 1853. But the end seemed near in early 2014, when the company that owned Scheltema went bankrupt. Luckily, it made a fresh start at a new location, and now has five floors filled with a staggering 120.000 books. That also includes second hand books, a fine selection of English and German literature, and a coffee bar on the first floor.

149 WATERSTONES

Kalverstraat 152
Old Centre ②
+31 (0)20 638 38 21
waterstones.com

Stepping into Waterstones is like stepping into an atmospheric old library, with personal tips from employees snuck in between the books. The store is housed in a monumental building by the Dutch architect H.P. Berlage, adjacent to 'book square' Het Spui, with its weekly book market on Fridays.

150 AMERICAN BOOK CENTER

Spui 12
Old Centre ②
+31 (0)20 625 55 37
www.abc.nl

It's easy to get lost as you wander through the bookcases in this four storey mecca of English language literature. ABC also has good sections on travel, fantasy and games, and organises regular lectures, meetings and exhibitions in their Treehouse located across the square at Voetboogstraat 11.

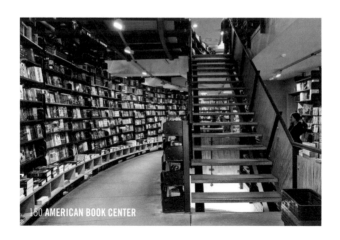

150 AMERICAN BOOK CENTER

The 5 best
SPECIALISED
BOOKSHOPS

151 REISBOEKHANDEL PIED À TERRE

Overtoom 135-137
West ④
+31 (0)20 627 44 55
www.piedaterre.nl

Globetrotters flock to this shop for travel guides, travel literature and all manner of maps: for cycling, hiking, climbing, driving and even flying. Browsing 400 square metre of books can be tiring. Luckily, there's a cafe in the back where they serve excellent coffee and apple pie.

152 LAMBIEK

Koningsstraat 27
Old Centre ②
+31 (0)20 626 75 43
www.lambiek.net

When the late Kees Kousemaker opened this shop in 1968, it was the first comic book store in Europe. It's since become world-renowned. Famous Dutch comic artists like Peter Pontiac and Joost Swarte started selling their work at this shop at a young age. Lambiek hosts regular exhibitions and also a yearly 24-hour comic day.

153 MENDO

Berenstraat 11
Negen Straatjes ①
+31 (0)20 612 12 16
mendo.nl

At Mendo, they know presentation is everything: here you'll find beautifully designed books on topics like photography, travel, design and architecture, displayed like works of art against walls made of black books. This sleekly designed space is pure eye candy, and the same goes for every book on sale here.

154 BOEKHANDEL ROBERT PREMSELA

Van Baerlestraat 78
Museum Q ③
+31 (0)20 662 42 66
www.premsela.nl

Looking out over the Museum square, this is an excellent place to browse for art books. There are three floors full of monographs, exhibition catalogues, books on art, graphic design, architecture and photography. The upstairs bargain section is always filled with a few gems.

155 PHOTOQ BOOKSHOP

Wijdesteeg 3-A
Old Centre ②
+31 (0)20 672 09 89
photoqbookshop.nl

Edie Peters, the founder of photography platform PhotoQ, opened this store in 2013. This 60-square-metre bookshop specialises in documentary and journalism photography, and offers beautifully designed books published by photographers themselves. Books can also be ordered online.

155 PHOTOQ BOOKSHOP

The 5 best
FOOD MARKETS

156 TEN KATEMARKT

Ten Katestraat
West ④
www.tenkatemarkt.nl

A daily neighbourhood market that's been around since 1912. Owing to the recent arrival of hipster hotspot De Hallen, it can get quite crowded on Saturdays. You'll find stalls selling cheap vegetables and fruits, cheese, fish, nuts, bread and according to some, the best hummus in town. Behind the stalls are some nice cafes, a tasty tapas bar and bargain antique shops.

157 LANDMARKT

Schellingwouder-
dijk 339
North ⑦
+31 (0)20 490 43 33
www.landmarkt.nl

A covered market hall that sells fresh and local produce. Landmarkt opened its doors in 2012 and recently expanded into the city with a smaller location in De Pijp. We still recommend going to Noord though, because it has a nice cafe and large sunny terrace in beautiful surroundings. Saunter past the beautiful old Dutch dike houses on the Schellingwouderdijk.

158 DAPPERMARKT

Dapperstraat
Oosterpark Q ⑤
www.dappermarkt.nl

One of Amsterdam's most multicultural markets, attracting visitors from far beyond the city. You can buy Surinamese, Antillean, Turkish, and Moroccan foods here, as well as some of the best fries and fish in town. Besides food, you'll find cheap clothing, shoes, housewares and fabrics. The streets surrounding Dappermarkt are worth exploring as well.

159 LINDENMARKT

Lindengracht
De Jordaan ①
www.jordaanmarkten.nl/
lindenmarkt.htm

At the end of the 19th century, the Lindengracht canal was filled in. Since then a fresh food market has been held here. Buy anything from *stroopwafels* to organic olive oil here, at far better prices than the organic farmer's market around the corner in Noordermarkt. Lindenmarkt makes for a nice Saturday morning stroll. Afterwards sit down in one of the lively Jordaan cafes.

160 ZUIDERMRKT

Johannes Verhulst-
straat / Jacob
Obrechtstraat
Museum Q ③
www.zuidermrkt.nl

ZuiderMRKT is a small organic market, run by a cooperative. It was founded in 2011 by three locals who noticed that grocers, butchers and bakeries were rapidly disappearing in their neighbourhood. This Saturday market is run by members who pay a yearly contribution. They buy their fruit and vegetables directly from local producers. But you can buy much more here, including organic bread, turkey eggs, homemade granola and freshly-made pasta.

The 5 best
VINTAGE CLOTHING
shops

---

161 BIS!

Sint Antoniesbree-
straat 25-A
Old Centre ②
+31 (0)20 620 34 67
www.bis-vintage.nl

Hidden under the arcades of Sint
Antoniesbreestraat, Bis! is really an
amalgam of three separate vintage
stores. Here you'll find old army gear
and navy classics, fabulous vintage
dresses, jumpers, shirts and hats from
the fifties, sixties and seventies for men
and women and lots of cool shoes and
bags. They sell good quality items.

162 LAURA DOLS

Wolvenstraat 7
Negen Straatjes ①
+31 (0)20 624 90 66
www.lauradols.nl

Laura Dols grew up as a hippie in
Amsterdam and started selling clothes in
Waterlooplein. In 1977 she moved to the
Negen Straatjes. If you're looking for
a spectacular party outfit, then this is the
store for you: lots of festive frocks and
gowns, stylish suits for men, and fun party
outfits for all ages.

163 ZIPPER

Nieuwe Hoogstraat 8
Waterlooplein Q ②
+31 (0)20 627 03 53
www.zipperstore.nl

Secondhand Levi's, leather jackets, hats, fur coats, boots and bags: Zipper has it all. Their two family-owned stores are usually packed to the brim, their prices remain friendly. Zipper also recycles clothing under their own design label Ultra Zipper.

164 LENA AMSTERDAM

Westerstraat 174
De Jordaan ①
+31 (0)20 789 17 81
www.lena-library.com

Amsterdam's first fashion library. Lena offers vintage design, sustainable fashion and clothes from up and coming designers. Become a member and borrow clothes at a set price per month. If you like it, keep it: most clothing is for sale as well.

165 1953 RETRO & CHIC

Staalstraat 2
Waterlooplein Q ②
+31 (0)6 249 33 582

Known as one of the smallest, but also one of the best vintage shops in town. Items are handpicked by the two owners and carefully displayed. Think velvet hats, lace shirts, pearl necklaces, high-waisted dresses and designer bags. They also have a nice collection of men's leather shoes.

The 5 best shops for
DUTCH DESIGN

166 &KLEVERING

Haarlemmerstraat 8
Haarlemmer Q ①
+31 (0)20 422 27 08
klevering.nl

&klevering was founded in Amsterdam in 1992 and wants to 'brighten up everyday life at home'. Think classic Delftware with a twist, as well as geometric designs and lively prints that are inspired by nature. They regularly partner with talented Dutch designers and also design for the Van Gogh Museum and the Rijksmuseum.

167 MOOOI

Westerstraat 187
De Jordaan ①
+31 (0)20 528 77 60
www.moooi.com

A showroom full of Marcel Wanders's exciting and visually overwhelming design. Besides Wanders's own work, the work of national and international contemporary designers is for sale in this 850-square-metre warehouse. Bring several credit cards, or just feast your eyes.

168 DROOG

Staalstraat 7-B
Waterlooplein Q ②
+31 (0)20 523 50 50
www.droog.com

The Amsterdam-based design studio Droog created its own world in Staalstraat. The shop is part of a complex with a hotel, gallery, library, spa and a coffee and tearoom overlooking an inner garden that's open to shop visitors. Droog is known for giving unusual, fun twists to everyday objects.

169 STORE WITHOUT A HOME

Haarlemmerdijk 26
Haarlemmer Q ①
www.storewithout
ahome.nl

This started out in 2010 as a pop-up store, subsequently drifted around the city, but ultimately found a permanent home in Haarlemmerdijk. They sell affordable and quirky design items, like paper mounted animal heads, or crumpled ceramics, by – mostly unknown – Dutch and international brands, independent labels and talented designers.

170 THE MAKER STORE

Hannie Dankbaar-
passage 39
West ④
+31 (0)20 261 76 67
themakerstore.nl

Ninety different local designers and makers sell their highly original objects here; think cutting boards made from local trees, Amsterdam board games, or necklaces shaped like Amsterdam's street pattern. You might spot one of the designers at work in 'the Maker Space'. Once a month there's a big indoor market where you can meet even more makers.

169 STORE WITHOUT A HOME

The 5 best shops for
DESIGNER CLOTHES

---

171 SALON HELEEN HÜLSMANN

Willemsparkweg 166
Museum Q ③
+31 (0)20 238 69 65
www.salonheleen
hulsmann.nl

Real fashion addicts know where to shop, at Heleen Hülsmann's. She sells second-hand designer items in her tastefully decorated salon. Hand-picked pieces from recent collections by Prada, Givenchy, Dries van Noten, Isabel Marant, Lanvin, Ann Demeulemeester, Stella McCartney, Marni, Céline and Acne, to name just a few. Visit the shop by appointment or browse the online store.

172 ALMOST NOT DONE

Beulingstraat 21-H
Old Centre ②
instagram.com/
almostnotdone

A shop that offers a platform for young creatives, with regular events and exhibitions. Almost Not Done sells interior design, art and clothing: a mixture of new and secondhand, from high fashion designers like Dries Van Noten and Raf Simons to streetwear. The shop's young owner Jeff Hoogendijk only sells what he likes.

173 PRJCT AMS

Gasthuismolen-
steeg 18
Negen Straatjes ①
+31 (0)20 330 73 11
www.prjctams.nl

PRJCT AMS sells fashionable men's clothing with a young urban twist. Think suede caps, sturdy boots and jeans, slick leather jackets and Palo Wood sunglasses. They carry their own label, as well as brands like Won Hundred and Vive l'Homme. They also have an in-store made-to-measure (suit) service.

174 LES DEUX FRÈRES

Rozengracht 58
Negen Straatjes ①
+31 (0)20 846 46 13
www.lesdeuxfreres.nl

This shop, which was started by two brothers, offers all the wardrobe essentials the modern man should have in his closet: elegant for office hours and casual for the weekend. Think slimline suits, cufflinks and bow ties, as well as sporty trainers, leather jackets and flannel check shirts.

175 ENNU

Cornelis Schuyt-
straat 15
South ⑥
+31 (0)20 673 52 65
www.ennu.nl

High-end fashion in an ultra-stylish store in one of Amsterdam's more upscale shopping streets. Ennu has been selling men and women's clothes by Isabel Marant, Maison Martin Margiela, Ann Demeulemeester, Balenciaga and Balmain since 2002.

The 5 most
UNUSUAL SHOPS

―――――

176 DE PINDAKAAS-WINKEL

Czaar Peterstraat 169
Oostelijke Eilanden ②
www.depindakaas
winkel.nl

The Dutch have a special relationship with *pindakaas* (peanut butter). Some people even take their favourite brand with them on holiday. Whereas there used to be only two types in the past, crunchy or smooth, you can now head to this store for ten homemade flavours: from caramel and sea salt to onion and garlic.

177 STOFFEN & SLOFFEN

Burgemeester
Tellegenstraat 41
De Pijp ③
+31 (0)6 216 86 942
www.stoffenensloffen.nl

This shop is an explosion of colour that is bound to make you smile. Stoffen & Sloffen (Slippers & Fabrics) has the largest collection of 1970s fabrics, an array of colourful Greek slippers with pompoms, and also sells vintage interior design. Check opening hours.

178 HET OUD-HOLLANDSCH SNOEPWINKELTJE

Tweede Egelantier-
dwarsstraat 2
De Jordaan ①
+31 (0)20 420 73 90
www.snoepwinkeltje.com

Mariska Schaefer grew up in her grand-mother's cake shop. In 2002, she opened her own, old-fashioned Dutch candy shop in the Jordaan. From behind the counter, she sells pieces of *zoethout* (liquorice), *stroopsoldaatjes* (syrup soldiers made of caramelised sugar) and other sweets.

179 **TERRA INCOGNITA**

Van Baerlestraat 77
Museum Q ③
+31 (0)20 673 83 93
www.terra
incognitas.com

Some of the fossils, meteorites, dinosaur fangs, shark's teeth and rare stones sold at Terra Incognita have made it into the collections of natural history museums. This tiny shop is near the Concert Hall and the Museum district, and sells small treasures, some of which are millions of years old. Prices range from two euros to hundreds or more.

180 **HET KLEINSTE HUIS**

Oude Hoogstraat 22
Old Centre ②
+31 (0)20 752 75 85
www.hetkleinstehuis.nl

It's easy to overlook the city's smallest house as it's just 2,02 metre wide. Inside you'll find a specialty tea shop that sells high quality teas and lovely treats such as chocolate, nougat and liqueur. What's more: there's a tiny hidden tea room on the first floor where you can have brunch or enjoy a high tea. Book ahead.

179 TERRA INCOGNITA

The 5 best
SHOE SHOPS

---

181 UNITED NUDE

Molsteeg 10
Old Centre ②
+31 (0)20 626 00 10
www.unitednude.com

The architectural shoe brand United Nude opened a flagship store in Amsterdam in 2009. The shop was designed by architect and the co-founder of the brand, Rem D. Koolhaas (a nephew of the other Rem Koolhaas). The shoes are displayed against a wall of changing led lights. The Möbius Mid and Eamz Bliss, both striking shoes because of their minimalistic heels, have become design classics.

182 FRED DE LA BRETONIÈRE

Utrechtsestraat 77
Canal Belt South ③
+31 (0)20 626 96 27
www.freddela
bretoniere.com

Shoes and bags designed to make you feel better, according to Fred de la Bretonière. He's been designing in Amsterdam since the early seventies and since then has branched out over the world. He uses supple but sturdy organic leather for his eponymously named brand as well as for his Shabbies Amsterdam and Fretons brands. The shoes are casual and comfortable, but retain a certain elegance.

183 TERRA

Reestraat 21
Negen Straatjes ①
+31 (0)20 638 59 13
www.terra
amsterdam.com

If you walk by this beautiful storefront, you might think this is a Spanish ceramics shop, but look carefully and you'll spot the beautifully handcrafted shoes among the colourful bowls and jugs. The owner travels to Spain a few times a year and always comes back with traditional, handcrafted and lovingly-made items in classic designs. Think brogues, desert boots, sturdy cowboy boots and espadrilles.

184 HESTER VAN EEGHEN

Hartenstraat 1
Negen Straatjes ①
+31 (0)20 626 92 11
www.hester
vaneeghen.com

Hester van Eeghen studied literature and law, but her real passion is leather. She started selling her handmade bags on the city streets, until she could afford her first shop in Hartenstraat. Her designs can be found in museums and design stores across the world. The shoes are elegant, colourful and one of a kind.

185 SUNIKA

Bilderdijk-
straat 102 HS
West ④
+31 (0)20 616 69 00
www.sunika.nl

Sunika (Japanese for sneaker) sells a carefully selected range of sleek sneaker styles, with colourful and limited-edition men's and women's sneakers by major brands such as Puma and Adidas and smaller labels such as Finnish Karhu and Danish Arkk.

The 5 best shops to buy
DENIM

---

186 DENHAM STORE 495

Hobbemastraat 8
Museum Q ③
+31 (0)20 681 35 24
*www.denham
thejeanmaker.com*

This is as much a museum for denim as it is a shop. Jeans are exhibited in glass cases, with explanations about the different phases of denim making. On top of this, jeans are featured in videos and photography. It's clear that Denham considers each pair of jeans a work of art. In the 'blue salad bar', customers can have their jeans customised.

187 TENUE DE NÎMES

Haarlemmer-
straat 92-94
Haarlemmer Q ①
+31 (0)20 331 27 78
www.tenuedenimes.com

This shop is named after the French city of Nîmes, which is believed to be the birthplace of denim. In their store, owners René and Menno combine the sturdiness of jeans, with the elegance of silk. Brands include the usual suspects like Lee and Levi's, but also Swedish (Denim Demon) and Japanese (Momotaro Jeans) brands, as well as a nice selection of limited editions.

188 G-STAR RAW

P.C. Hooftstraat 24-28
Museum Q ③
+31 (0)20 471 11 17
www.g-star.com

Jeans, everyone loves them, but everyone likes to wear them differently, according to G-Star. So the employees of this massive store on the corner of the upscale P.C. Hooftstraat are more than willing to help you choose the right fit, offering drinks and advice in between fittings. They also have a sustainable collection, made from organic cotton.

189 NUDIE JEANS

Hartenstraat 2
De Negen Straatjes ①
+31 (0)20 737 16 27
www.nudiejeans.com

Swedish brand Nudie's jeans, in organic cotton, are made to last. This flagship store on the Nine Streets offers free repairs for your Nudie jeans. Because we all know that a good pair of jeans is a friend for life. The store also sells secondhand jeans and will give you a discount on a new pair if you hand in your old one.

190 DENIM CITY STORE

Hannie Dankbaar-
passage 22
West ④
+31 (0)20 820 86 14
www.denimcity.org

This store inside the Hallen is part of an 'innovation campus', including a denim school and a research academy. Denim City is all about making better and more sustainable jeans. Browse the store, which sells over twenty high-end brands.

The 5 best
INDEPENDENT
RECORD STORES

191 CONCERTO

Utrechtsestraat 52-60
Canal Belt South ③
+31 (0)20 261 26 10
www.concerto.nl

If not the best, then at least the largest CD store. Five buildings have been joined to bring you the best in pop, classical, jazz, dance and world music. The service is expert and friendly. There's a coffee corner with very tasty *tosti's* (grilled sandwiches) and Turkish bread. There are regular in-store performances.

192 BACKBEAT RECORDS

Egelantiersstraat 19
De Jordaan ①
+31 (0)20 627 16 57
www.backbeat.nl

This is one of those little gems you'd easily walk by. Located in the Jordaan, Backbeat has been selling soul, funk, jazz and blues since 1988, on vinyl and CD, new and secondhand. The small store is well-stocked, and the friendly owners are more than willing to chat about music.

193 RUSH HOUR

Spuistraat 116
Old Centre ②
+31 (0)20 427 45 05
www.rushhour.nl

A music store and record label that specialises in dance and electronic music. It's a favourite haunt for DJs. They are experts in house, but also have a good collection of disco, funk and jazz music. Rush Hour started out as a mail-order business in 1996.

194 CHARLES MUZIEK

Weteringschans 193
Canal Belt South ③
+31 (0)20 626 55 38

The storefront may look outdated, but inside you'll find a treasure trove of classical music and tons of CDs stowed away in boxes and on shelves. The shop's owner Anna Wassenaar, who took over from the shop's founder Fred Charles in 1991, stocks everything from the Middle Ages to modern day classical music, and even sells ethnic music (don't use the term 'world music', or you'll be scolded).

195 DISTORTION RECORDS

Westerstraat 244
De Jordaan ①
+31 (0)20 627 00 04
www.distortion.nl

Another small record store in the Jordaan, but this one specialises in alternative music and is stocked to the hilt with (punk)rock, indie, jazz, funk, drum&bass, electronic music and reggae. Mostly vinyl, but also some CDs. Its owner Amond Spee calls Distortion a 'real underground shop'. He likes to be on top of new trends and has a very loyal clientele.

191 CONCERTO

The 5 best places to
RENT A BIKE

---

196 FIETSVERHUUR HET AMSTERDAMSE BOS

Bosbaanweg 1
Amstelveen (suburbs)
+31 (0)20 644 54 73
www.amsterdamsebos
fietsverhuur.nl

In the southwest of the city, you'll find 935 acres of green space and 51 kilometres of bike trails. The Amsterdamse Bos bike rental shop is a good place to start your visit. You can park your car for free and get a rental bike, or start with a drink on the patio of cafe De Boshalte.

197 HET ZWARTE FIETSENPLAN

Lijnbaansgracht 282
Canal Belt South ③
+31 (0)20 670 85 31
www.hetzwartefietsen
plan.nl

Het Zwarte Fietsenplan has several bike shops all over the city. The locations in Lijnbaansgracht and Nieuwezijds Voorburgwal 146 are the places to go if you want to rent a bike. All their shops are open seven days a week.

198 FIETSREPARATIE-FIETSENVERHUUR AMSTERDAM

Buiksloterweg 5-C
(Tolhuistuin Pavilion)
North ⑦
+31 (0)6 139 98 675
www.fietsreparatie
amsterdam.nl

Take the ferry behind Central Station and you'll be in Amsterdam North in a matter of minutes. This is a fairly large part of the city, but public transport is scarce. It's nicer to explore North and its surroundings by bike. Some destinations that are worth a visit are the picturesque Nieuwendammerdijk and nature reserve 't Twiske.

199 BIKE CITY

Bloemgracht 68-70
De Jordaan ①
+31 (0)20 626 37 21
www.bikecity.nl

If you don't want a rental bike that screams 'hello, I'm a tourist!', then go to Bike City in the Jordaan. They rent inconspicuous, typically Dutch bikes out of the basement of an old house on one of Amsterdam's most beautiful canals, Bloemgracht. Please note they may adjust their opening hours in winter.

200 STARBIKES RENTAL

De Ruyterkade 143
Oostelijke Eilanden ②
+31 (0)20 620 32 15
www.starbikes
rental.com

StarBikes Rental rents so-called 'granny bikes'. To stop these minimalistic bicycles just back-pedal. Also available are tandems, kids' bikes and bikes for disabled people. And if you ever need to wait: StarBikes also serves food and beverages.

196 FIETSVERHUUR HET AMSTERDAMSE BOS

The 5 best
FLOWER SHOPS

201 POMPON

Prinsengracht 8-10
De Jordaan ①
+31 (0)20 622 51 37
www.pompon.nl

Flowers aren't wrapped in cellophane here, but are lovingly folded into rice paper. Fresh flowers are delivered daily and arranged on site to suit the customer's demands. They can make opulent floral arrangements here, as well as modern 'less is more' bouquets.

202 AMSTERDAMFLORA

Eerste Constantijn
Huygensstraat 57
West ④
+31 (0)20 612 78 95
www.amsterdamflora.nl

A traditional flower shop that's been around for over twenty years. Their abundant display of colourful flowers in front of their big corner store livens up the whole street. They make flower arrangements for all occasions, and can also deliver fruit baskets and wine.

203 MC BLOOM

Beethovenstraat 13
South ⑥
+31 (0)20 662 97 80
www.mcbloom.nl

MC, or Marc and Cora Koningen, run a very pretty flower shop in Beethoven-straat. The little artworks in their window display are bound to lure you inside, where it is easy to get lost among the seductive floral arrangements. They specialise in cut flowers, but also sell plants and accessories for your home.

204 GERDA'S BLOEMEN EN PLANTEN

Runstraat 16
Negen Straatjes ①
+31 (0)20 624 29 12

A simple bunch of tulips in a vase? But you can do so much more with flowers. At Gerda's, flowers steal the show and the bigger, the bolder, the better. If you're looking for some show-stopping flower arrangements, this is the place to go. Just walking past their displays is a treat.

205 SHOP HORTUS BOTANICUS

Van der Boechorst-
straat 8
South ⑥
+31 (0)20 598 93 90
www.vrienden
vuhortus.nl

Amsterdam's second Botanical Garden was founded by the Free University in 1967. It spans an area of one hectare, and has over 10.000 different plants, various greenhouses and an interesting collection of Bonsai trees. The adjoining shop sells flower arrangements, orchids, seeds, gardening and landscape design books as well as homemade honeys, jams and chutneys. The garden and shop are open on weekdays.

204 GERDA'S BLOEMEN EN PLANTEN

The 5 best

NEIGHBOURHOOD

SHOPPING *streets*

---

206 CORNELIS SCHUYTSTRAAT

South ⑥

P.C. Hooftstraat is considered Amsterdam's smartest shopping street, but you could easily argue that Cornelis Schuytstraat is much more upmarket. It's not dominated by large chain stores, posh cars and tourists eagerly flashing their credit cards. Cornelis Schuytstraat has retained the look and feel of a neighbourhood shopping street. High-end boutiques comfortably sit next to a bakery or a grocery.

207 JAVASTRAAT

Indische Buurt ⑤

The Indische Buurt used to be one of Amsterdam's rougher neighbourhoods, but in recent years, things have changed and the young and creative eagerly flock to this still affordable part of town. Javastreet, the vibrant centre of this multicultural neighbourhood, is still a good combination of Turkish and Moroccan grocers and butchers, next to specialty coffee shops and burger bars. Let's hope it stays that way.

208 UTRECHTSESTRAAT

Canal Belt south ③

Equal parts cafes/restaurants and shops, Utrechtsestraat is always lively, day and night. You can find some good specialty shops here, like the Concerto music store and Studio Bazar for kitchen supplies, as well as some of Amsterdam's best traditional pubs. Lately, a lot of new (high end) fashion stores have opened here, making the street an exciting mix of old and new Amsterdam.

209 CZAAR PETERSTRAAT

Oostelijke Eilanden ②

The locals were rather surprised when Czaar Peterstraat was elected 'best shopping street' in 2015. Wasn't this a dark and dreary street after all? Well, things have changed and it is now larded with superb specialty shops (think peanut butter, cheese, sausages and oil, to name but a few), has some great vegetarian and vegan-friendly restaurants and the best 'wunderkammer' of Amsterdam: Het Schelpenmuseum.

210 GERARD DOUSTRAAT

De Pijp ③

Many new shops have popped up here, most of them with combinations with a woman's name, like Anna + Nina (concept store) and Charlie + Mary (fashion). As you edge closer to the Ferdinand Bol, the shops become more down to earth: a Spanish deli, a cheese shop and Amsterdam's biggest shop for cookware, Duikelman. End your shopping spree on one of the terraces in Gerard Douplein.

The 5 best
SECONDHAND
MARKETS

---

211 NOORDERMARKT ON MONDAY
MONDAY 9 AM TILL 1 PM
Noordermarkt
De Jordaan ①
www.noordermarkt-
amsterdam.nl

A lively and bustling market with stalls full of mostly secondhand clothing, hats, shoes and bags, and lots of antiques. It's not cheap, but if you haggle in a friendly way, it's still possible to find a good deal. This market is only on Monday mornings. Come early if you want to avoid the crowds.

212 BOOK MARKET AT THE SPUI
FRIDAY 10 AM TILL 6 PM
Spui
Old Centre ②
www.deboekenmarkt
ophetspui.nl

Every Friday 25 booksellers from across the country flock to the Spui to sell their wares. There are lots of secondhand and antique books, first and rare editions, as well as old prints, posters, pamphlets, maps and magazines. There is a good chance you'll find something special here.

213 KING'S DAY MARKETS
27 APRIL

Every year on King's Day, Amsterdam turns into one large open-air market. People empty their attics and basements and sell their stuff on the street. If you like bargain and treasure hunting, then go to the affluent streets in the Old-South quarter.

214 **WATERLOOPLEIN**

MONDAY THROUGH
SATURDAY
Waterlooplein
Waterlooplein Q ②

This used to be a daily market in the heart of the old Jewish quarter. It completely disappeared during WWII, but was later revived as a flea market. In the sixties and seventies, this market was world-famous. It still retains some of its old hippie vibe, with vintage clothing, semi-antiques and old records.

215 **IJ-HALLEN**

T.T. Neveritaweg 15
North ⑦
+31 (0)22 958 15 98
www.ijhallen.nl

With 750 stalls, this is certainly the largest flea market in Amsterdam. It's held one weekend every month in a former dockyard in Noord. In the summer season, stalls are both indoors and outside. Everything for sale here is secondhand. Professional traders and private individuals who've cleaned out their attics sell their wares here. You pay 5 euro admission.

212 FRIDAY BOOK MARKET AT THE SPUI

The 5 best
INTERIOR DESIGN
stores

---

216 NEEF LOUIS DESIGN

Papaverweg 46
North ⑦
+31 (0)20 486 93 54
www.neeflouis.nl

Neef Louis (cousin Louis) is the go-to
destination for vintage and industrial
design lovers, as they sell everything
you ever hoped to find at flea markets:
from Rietveld and Rob Parry chairs
to industrial-style lockers and operation
room lamps.

217 FEST AMSTERDAM

Van Woustraat 111
De Pijp ③
+31 (0)20 261 51 60
www.fest.
amsterdam.nl

Affordable Dutch design furniture with
a Scandinavian twist. FEST Amsterdam
was started in 2013 by owner Femke
Furnée who invites different designers to
contribute to the Fest brand. Think sturdy
but soft lounge sofas, lots of colourful
cushions and pillows as well as elegant
chairs and vases.

218 AARDE WERELDS WONEN

Westerstraat 10
De Jordaan ①
+31 (0)20 423 32 10
www.aardewerelds
wonen.nl

Aarde Werelds Wonen sticks to its core
business: selling antique and ageless
furniture from central Asian countries.
They sell beautiful handmade woollen
carpets and colourful fabrics, solid
wooden chests and cupboards, as well as
ceramics and jewellery. Everything is fair
trade here.

219 **HUTSPOT**

Van Woustraat 4
De Pijp ③
+31 (0)20 223 13 31
www.hutspot
amsterdam.com

Hutspot is a shop, gallery, work space and cafe in one. The three young owners created a platform for new talent and are constantly searching for interesting designers and artists, who exhibit their products in a shop within the shop. After opening their instantly successful store in Van Woustraat in 2012, Hutspot opened another location in Rozengracht.

220 **MOBILIA**

Utrechtsestraat 62-64
Canal Belt South ③
+31 (0)20 622 90 75
www.mobilia.nl

When you're a student living in a small room with furniture from flea markets, this is where you dream about shopping one day. Mobilia spans three floors and sells sleek high-end design furniture as well as more affordable items. The list of brands they sell is endless. Even if you're not looking to buy, it's pleasant.

219 **HUTSPOT**

5 times
COFFEE with
A TWIST

---

221 JOSÉ MOLLURA AMSTERDAM

Amstelveenseweg 274
South ⑥
+31 (0)6 241 09 295
www.jose-mollura.com

There are rumours that José Mollura not only sells the best coffee in Amsterdam, but has the best coffee full stop. Argentinian José actually discovered his predilection for coffee in Amsterdam where he became an award-winning coffee roaster. Not only does he sell fab coffees, but he also designs and sells his own leather bags, a craft he learned in India.

222 CUT THROAT BARBER & COFFEE

Beursplein 5
Old Centre ②
+31 (0)6 253 43 769
www.cutthroat
barber.nl

Located just off Dam Square, Cut Throat combines an old-fashioned barber shop with barista-made coffee. Although they like to fuss about trimming beards and using the right beard oils and pomades, they're less fussy when it comes to their coffee, offering a simple espresso-based menu, with beans sourced from a local Amsterdam roaster. No reservation needed, just walk in.

223 COTTONCAKE

Eerste van der
Helststraat 76
De Pijp ③
+31 (0)20 789 58 38
www.cottoncake.nl

Cottoncake is so pristinely white that you're almost afraid to drop a crumb of their homemade walnut-banana bread on the floor. The food and drinks in this excellent cafe are locally sourced and mostly organic, vegetarian and gluten free. Besides food, they also sell Scandinavian, Dutch and Spanish fashion brands, as well as their own fashion label and local art.

224 CLOUD GALLERY AMSTERDAM

Prinsengracht 276
De Jordaan ①
+31 (0)20 358 35 74
www.cloud
amsterdam.com

An art gallery where you won't be stared at and where you don't feel the need to make sensible remarks about art you barely understand. At Cloud Gallery Amsterdam it's actually nice to sit down and drink a coffee. Almost as much thought has gone into the single-estate coffee and the carefully selected teas by a prize-winning sommelier, as in the art on the walls.

225 TYPICA AMSTERDAM

Rokin 75 (basement)
Old Centre ②
www.typicacoffee.nl

Tucked away in the basement of the Made furniture store, you'll find a speakeasy coffee bar that caters to local coffee lovers who are 'in the know'. Rik Bullens trained as a barista in Australia and wants to single-handedly upgrade the Dutch coffee standard.

EYE FILMMUSEUM

40 BUILDINGS TO ADMIRE

The 5 most striking
MODERN BUILDINGS

226 EYE

IJpromenade 1
North ⑦
+31 (0)20 589 14 00
www.eyefilm.nl

Amsterdam isn't generally known for its bold modern architecture, but the new film museum on the northern shore of the River IJ changed that in 2012. The design by Delugan Meissl Architects is a striking white angular landmark and is meant to depict a transition from reality into cinematographic fiction. Enjoy the sweeping views from the terrace, and watch a movie or visit an exhibition inside.

227 PALACE OF JUSTICE

IJdok 20
Westelijke Eilanden ①

Another striking new building on the shores of the IJ. The law courts moved here in 2013. The offices and the courts are connected by a skyway. The building by Claus and Kaan architects is reminiscent of an impressive iceberg rising from the water. The courtyard is intimate, and because of the greenish glass, it's almost as if you're inside the ice.

228 OBA

Oosterdokskade 143
Oostelijke Eilanden ②
+31 (0)20 523 09 00
www.oba.nl

The new public central library is a seven-storey temple for book lovers. Architect Jo Coenen used natural stone, glass and wood in a design that juts out at different angles. Inside, the massive, bright space (28.000 square metres) is divided into differently shaped intimate 'rooms'. A wonderful place to quietly read a book. There are regular exhibitions. On the top floor is a restaurant with a terrace.

229 STEDELIJK MUSEUM

Museumplein 10
Museum Q ③
+31 (0)20 573 29 11
www.stedelijk.nl

The new grand entrée for the Stedelijk Museum, a seamless white addition to the historical building, won the design competition in 2004, but it was instantly nicknamed 'the bathtub' – not meant as a compliment. *The New York Times* called it a "ridiculous building" and an "oversized plumbing fixture". We suggest you go and see for yourself; in any case the museum shop that's housed in this new wing is definitely worth a visit – it has a great book collection.

230 THE ROCK

Claude Debussy-laan 80
South ⑥

In the Netherlands we have a saying 'hoge bomen vangen veel wind', which means 'the bigger they are, the harder they fall'. A saying that's applicable to Amsterdam's business centre the Zuidas, the home of leading banks and law firms in tall skyscrapers. The Rock, designed by Erick van Egeraat, is a striking vertical structure with an irregular rock-like top. People either hate it or love it.

5

TOWERS

to climb

---

231 KALVERTOREN

Singel 457
Canal Belt South ③
www.kalvertoren.nl

A shopping centre in busy Kalverstraat, close to Muntplein, which boasts several well-known chain stores. But few people know you can climb all the way up into the tower, where you'll find cafe-restaurant Blue with a 360° view over the city centre.

232 FLETCHER HOTEL SKY LOUNGE

Schepenbergweg 50
South-East (suburbs)
+31 (0)20 311 36 70
www.fletcherhotel
amsterdam.nl

There are not enough superlatives to describe the sky lounge on the 17th floor of the blue Fletcher tower. It has the highest view of Amsterdam, a whale shaped piano and a massive chandelier. Drink a cocktail here or have some sushi. Only drawback: it's located in a not so charming office area in the southeast.

233 WESTERTOREN

Prinsengracht 281
De Jordaan ①
+31 (0)20 689 25 65
www.westertoren
amsterdam.nl

With its red and blue roof, this is one of the most iconic towers of Amsterdam. Anne Frank wrote about her view of the tower from her room in her diary, and there are many classic Jordaan songs featuring the Westertoren. From April through October there are daily guided tours. It's also the highest tower (85m) in Amsterdam.

234 RANSDORPER TOREN

Durgerdammer-
dijk 63
North (Ransdorp) ⑦
+31 (0)20 490 46 05

Ransdorp is a village from the Middle Ages that was popular with seafarers. It was swallowed up by Amsterdam in 1921. The truncated Ransdorper tower dates from the sixteenth century and is the oldest remnant of the old village. It's open daily in summer, except for Mondays. The tower offers views of Amsterdam North, the River IJ and even IJburg.

235 A'DAM TOREN

Overhoeks
North ⑦
www.adamtoren.nl

North of the River IJ is where you'll find one of Amsterdam's most eye-catching towers. It was designed in the seventies by Arthur Staal for Royal Dutch Shell, and is still known as the Shell Tower. It remained vacant for several years, but in 2014 the renovation of the tower started. The building is now home to offices, music studios, clubs, a hotel and a revolving restaurant with an observation deck and swings on the rooftop.

233 **WESTERTOREN**

The 5 most iconic
AMSTERDAM SCHOOL
buildings

---

236 JERUZALEMKERK

Jan Maijenstraat 14
West ④
+31 (0)20 612 46 28
www.jeruzalem-kerk.nl

A completely symmetrical imposing red brick church with stained glass windows representing the seven days of creation. The building also comprises seven apartments. Here the church and houses are adjoined, so that God could be close to his people. Jeruzalemkerk was built in the late 1920s and is an early result of crowdfunding. It's especially beautiful when the sun sets. Enjoy the view from Cafe Cook's terrace.

237 DE DAGERAAD

P.L. Takstraat
South ③

The gracefully undulating curves of this building contrast beautifully with the small horizontally slatted windows. It was commissioned by the socialist housing corporation 'De dageraad' (The dawn), designed by Michel de Klerk and Piet Kramer and built in 1920. It had 294 apartments and several ground floor stores. In one of the old shops you'll find a visitor's centre that's open from Thursday till Sunday.

238 HET SCHIP

Oostzaanstraat 45
Westerpark Q ④
+31 (0)20 686 85 95
www.hetschip.nl

'Het Schip' (The ship) was built between 1914 and 1921 as a working man's palace. The three buildings comprise low-rent housing for labourers, a post office and a tower. In the Museum of the Amsterdam School for architecture that's located here, you can see an original labourer's home filled with period pieces, as well as the post office. The Ship was designed by Michel de Klerk and is considered one of the finest exponents of this architectural style.

239 VRIJHEIDSLAAN

Vrijheidslaan
South ③

Vrijheidslaan (Freedom Lane) is the eastern entrance to Berlage's Plan Zuid. At the end of the 20th century, this urban plan was implemented to end the housing shortage and improve the cramped living conditions in the city centre. There are many different examples of Amsterdam School architecture in this street, designed by a commission of 17 architects. After WWII it was briefly called Stalin Lane.

240 HET SIERAAD

Postjesweg 1
West ④
+31 (0)20 820 09 28
www.het-sieraad.nl

When 'Het Sieraad' (The Jewel) was built in the early 1920s it lay on the western edge of the city. This imposing structure was built on a pentagonal plot and has been home to several educational facilities since then. The facade is adorned by Hildo Krop's sculptures. Nowadays, it's still a school, but it also has a cafe-restaurant on the ground floor with a large waterfront terrace.

The 5 most striking
CANAL HOUSES

241 MUSEUM HET GRACHTENHUIS

Herengracht 386
Old Centre ②
+31 (0)20 421 16 56
www.hetgrachten
huis.nl

This stately building was designed in the 17th century by the famous architect Philip Vingboons and was the home of merchants and bankers. A lot of important financial deals were made here, with the Russian tsarist regime, the French monarchy and during the American War of Independence. It now houses the Museum of the Canals. Through an interactive exhibition you'll quickly become acquainted with the history of Amsterdam's canals, a UNESCO World Heritage site.

242 HUIS MET DE HOOFDEN

Keizersgracht 123
Old Centre ②
+31 (0)20 760 21 21
www.huismetde
hoofden.nl

Legend has it that a kitchen maid called Anna cut off the heads of six burglars who tried to get into the house through a kitchen hatch, hence the six heads on the building's facade. They are actually the heads of six Roman gods. This 17th-century house, designed by Hendrick de Keyser, was a haven for freethinkers and it is believed that Spinoza and Comenius visited here. Inside you'll find the library that inspired Dan Brown's books.

243 HUIS BARTOLOTTI

Herengracht 170-172
Old Centre ②

This is an elaborate Baroque house from the early 17th century. Huis Bartolotti is tucked away in a corner of Herengracht and was commissioned by one of the richest Amsterdammers, Willem van den Heuvel, who was said to have a fortune of 400.000 guilders. Although he largely owed his fortune to an inheritance, the façade bears Latin mottos such as 'through hard work' and 'religion and virtue'.

244 AMSTERDAM PIPE MUSEUM

Prinsengracht 488
Canal Belt South ③
+31 (0)20 421 17 79
www.pipemuseum.nl

This canal home now houses a pipe collection. It started in 1969 with an excavation along Keizersgracht where a lot of cafe waste was found, including clay pipes. This find sparked the interest of the amateur archeologist Don Duco. The museum now houses more than 30.000 objects from five continents. Downstairs is a shop, the museum is located in the 17th-century townhouse, with a beautiful interior and period furniture.

245 BIBLICAL MUSEUM

Herengracht 366-368
Old Centre ②
+31 (0)20 624 24 36
www.bijbelsmuseum.nl

The Biblical Museum is located in the Cromhout houses, named after the trader Jacob Cromhout who had them built in 1662. They were both designed by the architect Philips Vingboons, in a Classicist architectural style. If you look closely, you'll see a piece of bent wood in the building's façade. This is a reference to the inhabitant's name as Cromhout means bent wood in Dutch.

The 5 best
NEIGHBOURHOODS
to admire

---

246 BETONDORP

Watergraafsmeer ⑤
www.betondorp.nl

'Abandon all hope, he who grows up here', that's how the famous Dutch writer Gerard Reve described Betondorp. He wrote about this neighbourhood in his 1947 novel *De Avonden (The Evenings)*. Other famous inhabitants include the football player Johan Cruyff and the photographer Ed van der Elsken. The 1920s minimalist houses are built from cement because bricks were too expensive at the time. Betondorp inspired the German *Plattenbau*.

247 TUINDORP OOSTZAAN

North ⑦

This extension of the city was built around 1920 on the northern shore of the River IJ to provide housing for the growing population of labourers. In North, there were two large shipyards at the time. The workers lived nearby in these small low-rise houses, centred around Zonneplein. It's still a close-knit community, where you can still hear the real Amsterdam accent and dialect. There's a 1920s museum house on Meteorenweg 174.

248 IJBURG

Suburbs

IJburg is a string of artificial islands that are under construction, and showcases some of the best and worst in modern architecture. You'll find some surprising houses around Steigereiland Zuid where a lot of creatives built their homes. Check out the floating villas at Steigereiland Noord. At the far end of IJburg you'll find De Witte Kaap, Amsterdam's take on the Flatiron Building, near Blijburg beach.

249 GWL-TERREIN

Van Hallstraat /
Haarlemmerstraat
Westerpark Q ④
www.gwl-terrein.nl

In the mid-nineties, a car-free and eco-friendly neighbourhood was built on the former site of *Gemeentelijke Waterleiding* (the city's waterworks). Both the munici-pality and the neighbours wished to create sustainable homes in a healthy en-vironment: green roofs, recycle rainwater, and lots of green areas. Some of the old buildings have survived, such as the water tower and the machine room, where you'll find cafe-restaurant Amsterdam.

250 DUBBELTJESPANDEN

Mauritskade 29-54
Oosterpark Q ⑤
www.dubbeltjes
panden.nl

The 'Dubbeltjespanden' (dime buildings) are an early example of social housing in Amsterdam. This intimate row of houses (just off the busy Mauritskade) was built in 1870. The cheap but well-built homes provided an alternative to the overpriced hovels many labourers lived in at the time. They paid a dime every week to the first Dutch cooperative housing association. This street was completely renovated in 2012.

The 5 most
CROOKED HOUSES

―――――――

251 VIJZELGRACHT
Vijzelgracht 4-10
and 20-26
Canal Belt South ③

The construction of this underground
North-South line has exceeded every
planning and budget limit, and on top
of that, has caused a significant nuisance.
In 2008 and 2012, several monumental
17th-century houses along Vijzelgracht
sagged 15-23 cms because of the
construction work, forcing residents to
temporarily leave their homes.

252 SLUYSWACHT
Jodenbreestraat 1
Waterlooplein Q ②
+31 (0)20 625 76 11
www.sluyswacht.nl

This very crooked free-standing house was
built in 1695 as the lockkeeper's house,
opposite the Rembrandt House museum.
One of the oldest pictures of this lock was
painted by Rembrandt when he still lived
across from it. In the last twenty years
Sluyswacht has been a cafe.

253 BEGIJNHOF
Begijnhof 30
Old Centre ②
+31 (0)20 622 19 18
www.begijnhof
amsterdam.nl

This peaceful and secluded inner courtyard is right in the middle of the busy city
centre. Beguines, unmarried women who
cared for the sick and elderly, used to live
here from the 14th century onwards. If
you look closely, the houses look like a
row of crooked teeth.

254 ROKIN

Rokin 116
Old Centre ②

The buildings on Rokin used to be near the water, but this last section of the Amstel River was drained in the 1930s. A Persian rug store and an art dealer were initially located here. In 2003 the building was vacant and was squatted twice in a year. It has since been renovated, but has retained its distinctly crooked shape.

255 SPIEGELGRACHT

Spiegelgracht 6
Canal Belt South ③

This tiny house with its clock gable comfortably rests on its neighbour. The 17th-century Spiegelgracht, a canal opposite the Rijksmuseum, is lined with galleries, art shops and jewelleries, and has several crooked houses. Canal houses often leaned forward so their façades wouldn't be damaged when hoisting goods up into the attic.

252 SLUYSWACHT

The 5 most special
RELIGIOUS BUILDINGS

---

256 **VERMANING AAN HET MEERPAD**

Meerpad 7
North ⑦
+31 (0)20 623 45 88

The Mennonite community of Nieuwendam holds its services in the smallest church of Amsterdam. This tiny white building was built in 1843, after the faithful 'crowd-funded' a sum of 4000 guilders. It is so small, because at the time, there were only 50 Mennonites living in the villages of Buiksloot and Nieuwendam.

257 **PORTUGUESE SYNAGOGUE**

Mr. Visserplein 3
Plantage Q ②
+31 (0)20 531 03 10
www.jck.nl

The 17th-century interior of this synagogue is completely intact. It is also home to the Ets Haim Library, the oldest operating Jewish library in the world, which is home to thousands of rare books, prints and manuscripts. Buy one ticket to visit both the synagogue and the nearby Jewish Museum.

258 **WESTERMOSKEE**

Piri Reïsplein 101
West ④
+31 (0)6 222 522 22
www.westermoskee.nl

The French-Jewish architects Marc and Nada Breitman drew on Ottoman examples when designing this Turkish mosque, combining this style with the dark red bricks that are so popular in the Netherlands. The mosque opened in 2016 and the result is remarkable.

259 ONS' LIEVE HEER OP SOLDER

Oudezijds
Voorburgwal 38
Old Centre ②
+31 (0)20 624 66 04
www.opsolder.nl

Catholics were prohibited from saying Mass after the 16-century Reformation had raged through the northern part of the Netherlands. They convened in conventicles such as Ons' Lieve Heer op Solder (Our Lord in the Attic). When St. Nicholas's Church (opposite Amsterdam's Central Station) opened in 1887, the 'attic' was no longer used. Since then it has become a museum.

260 ZUIDERKERK

Zuiderkerkhof 72
Waterlooplein Q ②
+31 (0)20 308 03 99
*www.zuiderkerk
amsterdam.nl*

The Zuiderkerk was built between 1603 and 1611 in Renaissance style. Its location, a tiny yard, almost makes you forget how crowded the city centre can be. The carillon dates from 1511 and is the oldest of Amsterdam. Visitors can climb the 68-metre-high tower in summer or by appointment.

256 VERMANING AAN HET MEERPAD

The 5 most fascinating
GABLE STONES

261 THE FOX AND THE CRAB

Noordermarkt 39-40
De Jordaan ①

This is an 18th-century depiction of the fable of the fox and the crab. The fox wants to race the crab and thinks he will easily win, but the crab secretly holds on to his tail and wins the race. A story about pride preceding the fall. The gable was restored in 2009, giving the fox back his snout.

262 DIE VINDERS KAMER 1644

Oudezijds
Voorburgwal 274
Old Centre ②

The stone depicts three meat inspectors around a butchered cow. On the left side is a butchered sheep. Originally this gable stone was located in Sint Pieterspoortsteeg. A now demolished church was a large meat hall where the inspectors' guild convened. The stone was moved in 1944 and restored in 2008.

263 BURGERWEESHUIS / AMSTERDAM MUSEUM

Kalverstraat 92
Old Centre ②
+31 (0)20 523 18 22
www.amsterdam
museum.nl

The Burgerweeshuis is a former orphanage. The entrance on Kalverstraat has an elaborate gable. In the middle is a white dove, the symbol of the orphanage. Around it are seated eight orphans. The text, by poet and playwright Joost van den Vondel, summons passers-by to donate money to the orphanage.

264 DE GAPER (THE YAWNER)

AT: CAFÉ DE
VERGULDE GAPER
Prinsenstraat 30
De Jordaan ①
+31 (0)20 624 89 75
www.devergulde
gaper.nl

From the 17th century onwards, *gapers* (yawners) were attached to the front of an apothecary to draw customers. They depict a figure with an open mouth who's not actually yawning, but ready to take medicine. If you look closely you'll see that this *gaper* has a pill resting on his tongue. The *gapers* were often Moors, a reference to the exotic origin of the medicine.

265 IN OBJECTEN

Oude Braak 21
Old Centre ②

There are still craftsmen who make modern stones on demand, like Hans 't Mannetje. He spent some time training with the famous sculptor Hildo Krop, and has made hundreds of gable stones. The one at Oude Braak 21, the former site of a construction company, depicts an electric drill. Notice the tiny hole it has made in the right hand corner.

261 THE FOX AND THE CRAB

HORTUS BOTANICUS

50 PLACES
TO DISCOVER
AMSTERDAM

———————

The 5 most
PEACEFUL SPOTS

266 **HORTUS BOTANICUS**
Plantage Midden-
laan 2-A
Plantage Q ②
+31 (0)20 625 90 21
www.dehortus.nl

The botanical garden of Amsterdam University opened in 1638 and has over 4000 different plant species. This quiet and isolated green paradise was a centre for study and innovation. Take the first plant of the widely distributed Brazilian coffee: it was bred in the Hortus, after arriving in Amsterdam from the Middle East in 1706. The rare Victoria water lily is another eye-catcher.

267 **DE PAPEGAAI**
Kalverstraat 58
Old Centre ②
+31 (0)20 623 18 89
*www.nicolaas-
parochie.nl*

This tiny church, surrounded by high street shops, offers a silent refuge from the busy Kalverstraat. Its history goes back to the 17th century and the aftermath of the Reformation, when it was founded as a conventicle where Catholics could convene in silence. It was located behind a bird shop, hence the name 'De Papegaai' (the parrot).

268 ZEVENKEUR-VORSTENHOFJE

Tuinstraat 197-223
De Jordaan ①

These almshouses were built in the middle of the 17th century by elderly Roman-Catholic ladies of irreproachable conduct to accommodate the underprivileged. Several years ago, the houses were renovated and consolidated into 12 houses, which are rented out by a housing association.

269 ALLEMANSKAPEL SINT JORIS

Oudezijds
Achterburgwal 100
Old Centre ②
+31 (0)20 626 66 34

This chapel opened in 1977 in the basement of a former sex theatre in the Red Light District. The chapel is named after Saint George who beat the dragon. The owners stress that: "It's a symbol for the victory over the sex theatre and its transformation into a chapel." Nowadays, members of various religious denominations meet here.

270 HUIS TE VRAAG

Rijnsburgstraat 51
South ⑥
+31 (0)20 614 34 93
www.huistevraag.nl

Go through the iron gate of 'Huis te Vraag' (house to ask) cemetery and you'll find yourself in a different world. The gravestones are overgrown, and there's nothing but silence. An inn was located here in the Middle Ages. Word has it that Emperor Maximilian I stopped there to ask the way to Amsterdam when he was travelling from Haarlem in 1489. Hence the name. Closed during weekends.

The 5 most exceptional
VIEWPOINTS

271 **RAMADA HOTEL**

Staalmeesters-
laan 410
New-West ④
+31 (0)20 570 53 72
*www.ramada-
amsterdam.com*

This restaurant and skybar is located on the 17th floor of the Ramada Hotel near Rembrandt Park. The hotel is located on the fringe of the inner part of the city and the post-war suburbs of New-West. From the top of this hotel, you can easily spot the differences between pre- and post-war Amsterdam.

272 **CANVAS OP
DE ZEVENDE**

Wibautstraat 150
Oosterpark Q ⑤
+31 (0)20 261 21 10
www.volkshotel.nl

Canvas is a club and restaurant on the seventh floor of what used to be the editorial office of the Dutch daily, *de Volkskrant*. The large windows of this old installation room offer a 360-degree view over the city.

273 **SILODAM**

Westelijke Eilanden ①
www.silodam.nl

Silodam is a block of flats with a terrace that offers a tremendous view of the River IJ. The large stone structure next to the dam used to be a grain silo that was built in the late 19th century. It was squatted in the 1980s and as such saved from demolition. It's now a national monument.

274 RESTAURANT STORK

Gedempt Hamer-
kanaal 201
North ⑦
+31 (0)20 634 40 00
www.restaurantstork.nl

Fish Restaurant Stork is located in 'De Overkant' (the other side), a former industrial area in Amsterdam North, with a great view of the River IJ. The area was once used by engine manufacturers, among which was Stork. It was recently rebuilt as a multi-purpose venue, but the industrial feel remains.

275 OKURA BAR AND RESTAURANT

Ferdinand
Bolstraat 333
De Pijp ③
+31 (0)20 678 71 11
www.okura.nl

Twenty Third in De Pijp is Hotel Okura's champagne and cocktail bar on the 23rd floor. From this centrally-located neigh-bourhood you can see the entire city. Here you'll also find Ciel Bleu, a two Michelin star-restaurant under the supervision of chef Onno Kokmeijer.

272 CANVAS OP DE ZEVENDE

The 5 most
BEAUTIFUL STREETS

---

276 NIEUWENDAMMER-DIJK
North ⑦

The lucky people living here are keen to point out that their street really is a village within the city. This dike was built in 1516 and seamen and captains used to live in the charming wooden houses with clock gables. It still has a historical feel to it though, contrasting beautifully with the more modern parts of North.

277 VESPUCCISTRAAT
West ④

This 1920s street with its Amsterdam School architecture is definitely worth walking through it. The red houses with symmetrical brick patterns seem to cast a warm glow, especially in the late afternoons. The street is lined with Japanese Ginkgo trees.

278 HENRI POLAKLAAN
Plantage Q ②

This street in the old Jewish quarter has a hushed grandeur, with 19th-century stately buildings and majestic trees. It was named after Henri Polak (1868-1943), a social democrat and chairman of the diamond workers union. The architect H.P. Berlage designed their headquarters at Henri Polaklaan 9, which you can visit (see: *www.deburcht.nl*).

279 RINGDIJK

Watergraafsmeer ⑤

The 17th-century Ringdijk is one of the dikes that prevents Watergraafsmeer (a *polder* 5 metres below sea level) from flooding. Walking across the green dike, you look down on the typical dike houses. At the corner with Middenweg there's an old courthouse (1777). It was here that Emperor Napoleon was offered the keys to Amsterdam when he visited in 1811.

280 BROUWERSGRACHT

De Jordaan ①

Connoisseurs know this is the most beautiful canal of them all. Eight bridges span Brouwersgracht, a canal in De Jordaan that's still lined with old warehouses with wooden shutters. *Brouwersgracht* (Brewer's canal) was named after the many beer brewers established here in the 16th and 17th centuries.

279 RINGDIJK

The 5 most
UNUSUAL FOUNTAINS

281 TAYOUKEN PISS
Groesbeekdreef
Southeast (suburbs)

Under a bridge in De Bijlmer, the 1960s southeast extension to the city, you will see six brightly coloured peeing men. 'Les pisseurs d' Amsterdam' is their name. They are the spitting image of the Cameroon-Belgian artist Pascale Tayou, who created this fountain in 2009 for an art event. The six peeing men have become favourites with the local community and were cleaned and restored in 2014.

282 MAN EN SCHAAP
Zeeburgerdijk /
Flevoparkweg
Indische Buurt ⑤

This bronze statue, 'Man and sheep', won the 2011 Amsterdam street art prize. It was designed by Merijn Bolink in 2003 and features a man and a sheep staring at each other just above the water line. Two jets of water spout from the man's eyes into the sheep's face.

283 SNOW WHITE AND THE SEVEN DWARFS

Frederiksplein
Canal Belt South ③

This is a well-known fountain, not in the least because people throw soap into the fountain, creating big flocks of foam – but not many people know it's actually called Snow White and the Seven Dwarfs. Snow White is the big spout in the middle, the seven dwarfs surround her. Even though the fountain is on a busy traffic intersection, it's a popular spot for cooling and calming down.

284 MAN URINATING IN PUBLIC

IJsbaanpad 50 /
ASV Arsenal
South ⑥

When cycling past football club Arsenal, you always end up doing a double take: is that really a man peeing from the sideline? The peeing footballer is a symbol for the Saturday afternoon player that can't hold in his pee, and was designed by Erik Kessels for a 2011 art exhibition that was held at the ASV Arsenal grounds.

285 HOGEWEG FOUNTAIN

Hogeweg /
Linnaeusparkweg
Watergraafsmeer ⑤

From 1900 to 1932, a cast-iron fountain stood at this charming roundabout in Watergraafsmeer. The neighbours actively lobbied to have a new flat round fountain with several spouts installed here in 2007. Not everyone was happy though. One neighbour complained about the noise of the water and even sued the city but eventually gave up and moved. The benches around the fountain are a popular meeting place and children like to frolic in the water in summer.

The 5 best
HIDDEN GARDENS

286 NATUURTUIN SLATUINEN

Slatuinenweg 45
West ④
+31 (0)20 412 43 61
www.natuurtuin
slatuinen.wixsite.com/
slatuinen2

Slatuinenweg is a peculiar and narrow 17th-century path, that used to be lined with vegetable patches (*slatuinen* means salad gardens), but now is lined with highly sought-after historic low-rise houses. Behind number 45 is a well-kept secret: a natural garden with some forest, a marsh and ponds. This green paradise is open to the public on Thursdays and every first Sunday of the month.

287 ORANJEKERK GARDEN

Tweede van
der Helststraat 1-3
De Pijp ③
+31 (0)20 679 55 59
www.oranjekerk
amsterdam.nl

Right next to the protestant Oranjekerk, in the heart of the densely built De Pijp, is a biblical church garden with plants bearing names like Honesty, Jacob's ladder and Solomon's seal. There's also a grape arbor and a frog pond. Common swifts nest in the Oranjekerktower. The garden is open on Monday, Wednesday and Friday afternoons, and on Sundays after service.

288 HOTEL ARENA WITH MARIA CAVE

's-Gravesandestraat 51
Oosterpark Q ⑤
+31 (0)20 850 24 00
www.hotelarena.nl

The four-star Hotel Arena is housed in a monumental building which used to be Saint Elizabeth House for the chronically ill. It's located next to Oosterpark and has an adjoining garden. In a secret hidden corner, behind some bushes is a small man-made cave with a statue of Maria inside it, possibly put there for the sick to pray to. If you can't find it, ask at the reception.

289 TOLHUISTUIN (GARDEN)

Tolhuisweg 3
North ⑦

In the 19th century, this park was a popular destination for neighbourhood dwellers who even organised open-air concerts there. When Royal Dutch Shell bought up the entire area in the 20th century, the garden became a private garden. Shell employees grew vegetables here during WWII. The park was recently re-opened to the public.

290 VAN BRIENENHOFJE

Prinsengracht 85-133
De Jordaan ①

Arnaut van Brienen bought a house, a warehouse and beer brewery named 'De Star' in 1797 and broke them down to replace it with this *hofje*. He sadly died before the first stone was laid. The homes and large chapel are centred around a green courtyard with a water pump and a lantern in the middle. Van Brienenhofje used to be exclusively for Roman Catholics, but this strict condition no longer applies.

The 5 most
CHARMING SQUARES

---

291 ZONNEPLEIN
North ⑦

Zonneplein is the central square of Tuindorp Oostzaan, a working-class neighbourhood built in the 1920s. In addition to some shops, you'll also find Zonnehuis in the square, a theatre and former meeting place for workers' associations. It was built in the Amsterdamse School architectural style in 1932.

292 KADIJKSPLEIN
Plantage Q ②

Kadijksplein is located on a dike that protects the Plantage Quarter from the River IJ. Several trees in this charming square provide some shade. It also has a tiny terrace. In the middle of the square stands a statue of a seaman, looking at a building that used to be the sailor's home.

293 KASTANJEPLEIN
Oosterpark Q ⑤

Amsterdam isn't known for its attractive squares, but Kastanjeplein definitely is the exception to the rule. Fourteen old *kastanjebomen* (chestnut trees) create some shade. The original, cast-iron Ritter lampposts still light up the square when evening falls.

294 AMSTELVELD

Canal Belt South ③

Originally a large church was supposed to be built in Amstelveld in the 17th century. Ultimately, however, the tiny, wooden Amstelkerk was built instead. It was supposed to be a temporary structure, but has survived. Because of the small church, the square remained very spacious. Dozens of wingnuts surround the football pitch in the middle. There's a flower market on Mondays and also the occasional antique market.

295 ARTISPLEIN

Plantage Q ②
www.artis.nl/artisplein

Artis recently opened a small part of the zoo to the general public. Artisplein is a freely accessible square where you can smell the animals, spot the flamingos and observe birds from the Dutch polder in the neighbouring aviary. Can you think of a better way to escape the city?

293 KASTANJEPLEIN

The 5 most

UNUSUAL SCULPTURES

---

296 OFFICE WORKERS
Schalk Burger-
straat 1-2a
Oosterpark Q ⑤

On the ledge of this block of houses and offices you can spot a small procession of bronze office workers, suitcases in hand. The work was created in 2002 by Elisa van Schie and Martin Takken and commissioned by the housing association Woningbedrijf Amsterdam (now Ymere).

297 HOW TO MEET AN ANGEL
Eerste Constantijn
Huygenstraat 38
West ④

Look up when you pass the Mentrum psychiatric centre. You'll see a ladder sticking out from the roof and at the end of it a person reaching towards heaven. 'How to meet an angel' was designed by the Russian-American couple Ilya and Emilia Kabakov. This statue is about hope and the gradual healing process.

298 MAN WITH VIOLIN CASE
Tweede
Marnixplantsoen
De Jordaan ①

In 1982, this was the first anonymous statue to suddenly appear in the middle of the night. This headless man holds a violin case and seems to be running to catch his tram, keeping his hat in place with one hand. Over the years, it has been repainted several times. After protests, it was repainted in the original navy blue.

299 **BREAST PLATE**
Oudekerksplein
Old Centre ②

In February 1993, this copper-plated breast and hand suddenly appeared in Oudekerksplein. The municipality removed the illegally placed piece of art. A difficult job as it was cemented onto the ground. If the artist made himself known, the breast plate would be returned to its former position. He did contact the town council but has chosen to remain anonymous to this day.

300 **ZAGERTJE**
Leidsebosje
Canal Belt South ③

This sculpture is bound to put a smile on your face, if you know where to find it. It's in a small patch of green that is known as Leidsebosje (next to Café Americain in Leidseplein). On top of a tree branch is a small figure, sawing away. It's another anonymously placed work of art, which appeared in 1989.

300 ZAGERTJE

The 5 most unexpected places in
VONDELPARK

301 CENTRUM DE ROOS

P.C. Hooftstraat 183
Museum Q ③
+31 (0)20 689 00 81
www.roos.nl

De Roos is a centre for mindfulness and spirituality and was founded in 1984. Their patio or sun porch is a great place to stop for a coffee, a sandwich or a slice of freshly-baked apple pie. The centre is located near the park exit leading to chique Pieter Cornelisz Hooftstraat.

302 VONDELKERK

Vondelstraat 120
South ⑥

Architect Pierre Cuypers placed Vondel-kerk (Vondel church) right in the middle of Vondelstraat. The church was built in 1872 in a neo-Gothic architectural style. After WWII, it fell into disrepair. The diocese sold it to an investor for one euro. In 1984, squatters moved in, saving the church from demolition. It was later renovated.

303 STORKS

Island in the park
South ⑥

The stork population reached a critical level several decades ago. To prevent the species' extinction, environmental groups started breeding projects and helped the birds to find nesting sites. Vondelpark has an artificial nest. It's fenced off for visitors, but they can't be missed. You'll easily spot them from the rose garden.

304 VONDELBUNKER

Vondelpark 8
(under the bridge)
South ⑥
www.vondelbunker.nl

Not much is known about the atomic bunker under the bridge connecting Eerste Constantijn Huygenstraat and Van Baerlestraat. It was built in the 1940s and subsequently became a music centre for hippies and squatters. Even Pink Floyd performed here. It's now a rehearsal space, bar, and an arts and debating centre.

305 PICASSO'S 'FIGURE DÉCOUPÉE (L' OISEAU)'

South ⑥

Pablo Picasso donated this statue of a fish-like bird to the city of Amsterdam, on the condition that the artwork would be permanently exhibited in the park. It was a gift to celebrate the centennial of Vondelpark in 1965. There were plans to sell the artwork in 1994 and to use the money to pay for the maintenance on the park, but these plans were withdrawn.

305 PICASSO'S
FIGURE DÉCOUPÉE (L' OISEAU)'

The 5 most beautiful
B R I D G E S

---

306 VIERWINDSTREKEN-BRUG

Jan van Galenstraat /
Admiralengracht
West ④

'The four cardinal directions' Bridge
was built in 1925. Its corners feature an
Eskimo with a seal and walrus (North),
a Chinese man with boats (East), an
African with a spear and shield and two
lions (South) and an American with a
telephone and automobiles (West), all
designed by Hildo Krop (1884-1970).

307 PYTHON BRIDGE

Panamakade /
Stuurmankade
Oostelijke Eilanden ②

Two spectacular red, bent steel bridges
where designed by Adriaan Geuze in the
Eastern dock area. The largest of the two
writhes like a snake and is nicknamed
'Python bridge'. The low bridge is wheel-
chair-accessible and prevents ships from
hitting the underlying Piet Hein Tunnel.

308 KOEKJESBRUG

Bosboom Toussaint-
straat / Nieuwe
Passeerdersstraat
Canal Belt South ③

Koekjesbrug was built in 1911 to connect
the new working class area in Amsterdam
West to the city centre. Nobody knows
what *koekjes* (cookies) refers to, but writer
Martin Bril wrote a short story about it.
'It's a beautiful, old bridge, and I like the
name, for a bridge. Every time I cross it,
I mutter it swiftly: Koekjesbrug.'

309 NIJLPAARDENBRUG

Plantage Doklaan /
Entrepotdok
Plantage Q ②

Nijlpaardenbrug or Hippopotamus Bridge is a red, yellow and blue drawbridge which dates from 1987. The view of the old buildings is nice, but it's best to approach the bridge from the other side, so you can see the African savannah of Artis with its zebras and oryxes.

310 DRIEHARINGENBRUG

Prinseneiland /
Bickerseiland
Westelijke Eilanden ①

The three Westelijke eilanden (Bickers-eiland, Realeneiland and Prinseneiland) are a beautiful historic part of Amsterdam, dating from the early 17th century. You'll see a lot of converted old warehouses here where merchants used to store herring, grain and tobacco, among other things. The islands are connected by a series of bridges, the smallest being Drieharingenbrug (Three herring bridge). It's a wooden drawbridge for pedestrians and cyclists only.

307 PYTHON BRIDGE

The 5 best places to find
STREET ART

311 KEITH HARING
Jan van Galenstraat 4
West ④

Well, this literally is a hidden secret. On a wall of the wholesale market Food Center Amsterdam you can see a mural by Keith Haring which he completed in 1986. To protect this gigantic piece of art it has been covered up, but now that the Food Center is being redeveloped, Haring's cheerful monster will be revealed again. The expected year of completion is 2034.

312 THE LONDON POLICE
Prinsengracht /
Tuinstraat
De Jordaan ①

On the corner of Prinsengracht and Tuinstraat, close to GO Gallery, is an impressive sky-high mural by a couple of street artists known as The London Police. Their black and white graphic style with round figures is instantly recognisable. It was commissioned by the owner of the house.

313 HUGO KAAGMAN
Hemonylaan
De Pijp ③

Hugo Kaagman has been stencilling the streets of Amsterdam since the late seventies, developing a unique style. His Moorish and Delft Blue motifs have become commercially succesful. In Hemonylaan in De Pijp, he has a 'practice wall' (roughly opposite the houses at number 7 through 11).

314 RUA
Havenstraat
South ⑥

The Brazilian street art collective Reflexo on Urban Art (RUA) has been commissioned to create several large murals in Amsterdam. You'll find a lot of them in the South-East H-neighbourhood. Although made by different artists, you can recognise the bold use of colours and imaginative figures. Across from the Haarlemmermeer tram depot is a massive mural by Rimon Guimarães.

315 VARIOUS ARTISTS
Zeeburgerdijk /
Zeeburgerbrug
Indische Buurt ⑤

Venture out to the far East. On the walls of 209 and 211 Zeeburgerdijk you can spot the work of several (inter)national graffiti and stencil artists. It's only a prelude to what you'll find on the columns of Zeeburgerbrug: this is a so-called legal graffiti zone, so you can always spot artists at work during the day.

312 THE LONDON POLICE

ANNET GELINK GALLERY

60 PLACES
TO ENJOY CULTURE

The 5 most inspiring
MUSEUMS

—————————

316 HUIS MARSEILLE

Keizersgracht 401
Old Centre ②
+31 (0)20 531 89 89
www.huismarseille.nl

When Huis Marseille opened its doors in 1999, it was the first museum for photography in the Netherlands. Located in a beautiful old canal house with six rooms, it's recently been upgraded and extended. Major alternating exhibitions, with an emphasis on documentary photography from around the world.

317 KATTENKABINET

Herengracht 497
Canal Belt South ③
+31 (0)20 626 90 40
www.kattenkabinet.nl

Bob Meijer turned this 17th-century canal house into a museum devoted entirely to cats. It was founded in 1990 in memory of Meijer's own red tomcat, John Pierpont Morgan. His feline friend is featured in several works of art. The museum furthermore boasts paintings by Henry Toulouse-Lautrec, Sal Meijer, Pablo Picasso and Joseph Steinlen. Oh, and some live cats as well.

318 NIEUW DAKOTA

Ms. van
Riemsdijkweg 41-B
North ⑦
+31 (0)20 331 83 11
www.nieuwdakota.com

This contemporary art exhibition space hosts new solo and group exhibitions almost every month. The organisation often cooperates with external curators, cultural institutions and artists. You'll find Nieuw Dakota in one of the silos in the NDSM shipyard in Amsterdam North, next to the ferry station. Open from Thursday till Sunday.

319 HOUSE BOAT MUSEUM

Prinsengracht 296-K
De Jordaan ①
+31 (0)20 427 07 50
*www.houseboat
museum.nl*

Up until the sixties, the 'Hendrika Maria' used to carry sand and gravel. But her cargo days are over, and she has been converted into a house boat. The boat's owner Vincent van Loon noticed how tourists were always curious to see his houseboat, so he turned it into a museum. Walking through the cosy fifties interior, it's as if the owners have only just popped out for groceries.

320 STADSARCHIEF

Vijzelstraat 32
Canal Belt South ③
+31 (0)20 251 15 11
*www.stadsarchief.
amsterdam.nl*

Everything you ever wanted to know about Amsterdam is kept in the city archives: millions of maps, 50 kilometres of archives, and extensive film and photo documents. The Amsterdam City Archives host regular exhibitions, but don't forget to visit the permanent collection in the basement of this massive former bank building: lots of hidden secrets behind thick, steel-plated safe doors.

The 5 best
ART GALLERIES
in De Jordaan

---

321 TORCH GALLERY

Lauriergracht 94
De Jordaan ①
+31 (0)20 626 02 84
www.torchgallery.com

When the late Adriaan van der Have founded TORCH gallery in 1984, he was one of the first to introduce contemporary photography as an art form in the Netherlands. TORCH hosts about eight exhibitions a year in its gallery in the Jordaan district. Past exhibitions featured the work of Inez Lamsweerde, Anton Corbijn, Victor&Rolf, Takashi Murakami and Leni Riefenstahl.

322 GALERIE WOUTER VAN LEEUWEN

Hazenstraat 27
De Jordaan ①
+31 (0)6 520 31 540
www.wouter vanleeuwen.com

Tucked away in the 'gallery alley' of De Jordaan is Galerie Wouter van Leeuwen. For the past 14 years, Van Leeuwen has been promoting the work of young and established international photographers. The gallery specialises in contemporary photography, ranging from autonomous work to documentary photography. Past exhibitions included the work of Ellen von Unwerth, Paul Huf, Han Singels and Michael Wolf.

323 GALERIE RON MANDOS

Prinsengracht 282
De Jordaan ①
+31 (0)20 320 70 36
www.ronmandos.nl

Step into this spacious gallery with white walls and high ceilings, and it's as if you've been transported to New York's Meatpacking District. Here, Ron Mandos shows the work of up and coming contemporary artists. He is known for his annual exhibitions of the best work of Rijksacademie graduates. Mandos is also a staunch promoter of video art: in the past 13 years he has hosted at least 20 video art exhibitions.

324 GO GALLERY

Prinsengracht 64
De Jordaan ①
+31 (0)20 422 95 80
www.gogallery.nl

The owners Oscar van der Voorn and Farud Cambatta are devoted to promoting the work of graffiti and street artists, showing the work of Amsterdam based artists Ives.One, Kamp Seedorf, Zaira and Max Zorn. The GO gallery commissions art works for public spaces as well. Next door to their gallery you can see a massive mural made by duo The London Police.

325 ANNET GELINK GALLERY

Laurierstraat 187-189
De Jordaan ①
+31 (0)20 330 20 66
www.annetgelink.com

Since opening in 2000, Annet Gelink soon emerged as one of the leading forces on the contemporary art scene, participating in all major international art fairs such as Art Basel, Art Basel Miami Beach and Frieze Art Fair. Gelink also promotes the work of talented young artists such as Yael Bartana, David Maljkovic and Ryan Gander. A new gallery space next door showcases the archives of photographer Ed van der Elsken.

The 5 best
CINEMAS

---

326 THE MOVIES

**Haarlemmer-
dijk 161-163
Haarlemmer Q ①
+31 (0)20 638 60 16
*www.themovies.nl***

The Movies was founded in 1912 and is the oldest cinema in town. Although additions were made to the building throughout the years, the building still exudes an early 20th-century cinema feel, especially in the art deco-style Room one. Head to the Movies for art house (light) films and its nice cafe and restaurant.

327 DE UITKIJK

**Prinsengracht 452
Canal Belt South ③
+31 (0)20 223 24 16
*www.uitkijk.nl***

De Uitkijk was founded in 1929. The building had been a cinema for some time, but its director Mannus Franken wanted to turn it into 'a cinema that shows art instead of entertainment' after he was inspired by the avant-garde art cinemas of Paris. Nowadays, this small cinema is run by a group of enthusiastic students programming films for connoisseurs.

328 LAB111

Arie Biemond-
straat 111
West ④
+31 (0)20 616 99 94
www.lab111.nl

The Wilhelmina Gasthuis was a hospital that opened in 1893. After its closure in 1983 it became a residential area but the 'W.G.-terrein' also has work spaces for artists. The former pathological anatomy laboratory was converted into LAB111, a cinema which often has a completely different programme from other local cinemas as well as a cafe, and a restaurant that offers a discount when you show your movie ticket.

329 RIALTO

Ceintuurbaan 338
De Pijp ③
+31 (0)20 676 87 00
www.rialtofilm.nl

Rialto is a neighbourhood cinema in the heart of De Pijp. It mainly screens European and non-Western films. Special programmes are organised on topics such as world cinema, classics, and films for children.

330 STUDIO K

Timorplein 62
Indische Buurt ⑤
+31 (0)20 692 04 22
www.studio-k.nu

Studio K belongs to the Kriterion foundation, a student organisation with roots in the Second World War resistance. Just like Kriterion (at Roetersstraat 170), Studio K is run by students. The foundation's initial goal was to contribute to students' independence by allowing them to work for their own money. The foundation also runs a gas pump, a restaurant and a child-care service.

5 (former)
BATHHOUSES

---

331 MUSEUM AMSTERDAM NOORD

Zamenhofstraat 28-A
North ⑦
+31 (0)6 821 91 182
www.museum
amsterdam noord.nl

There used to be quite a stigma on Amsterdam North. Some even called it 'Amsterdam's Siberia'. The tide has changed however. In 2009 the first museum about the history of this part of town opened its doors. It's located in the former bathhouse of the charming garden city of Vogeldorp.

332 BADHUIS JAVAPLEIN

Javaplein 21
Indische Buurt ⑤
+31 (0)20 665 12 26
www.badhuis-
javaplein.com

The bathhouse in Amsterdam East's Javaplein opened in 1942 and became a meeting place for local residents. After it closed in 1982, it was a Hindu temple for some time, and a shop specialised in recycled goods. Now it's a restaurant for lunch and dinner.

333 BADHUISTHEATER

Boerhaaveplein 28
Oosterpark Q ⑤
+31 (0)6 111 73 324
www.badhuistheater.nl

The bathhouse in Boerhaaveplein in Amsterdam east was built in 1921, in the Amsterdam School architectural style. Men and women entered the building separately. In 1985, when the bathhouse was under threat of demolition, the owner Mike founded a small and lively community theatre.

334 BADHUIS EN SAUNA DA COSTA

Da Costakade 200
West ④
+31 (0)20 612 59 46
www.badhuisdacosta.eu

The first bathhouse at Da Costakade opened in 1903 at number 150. It was demolished in 1968 and reopened on its current location. It was the last public bathhouse to be built by the municipality. In the eighties, the bathhouse was under threat of closing down. A group of volunteers saved it however. It is still open today.

335 SPLENDOR AMSTERDAM

Nieuwe Uilenburger-
straat 116
Waterlooplein Q ②
+31 (0)20 845 33 45
www.splendor
amsterdam.com

A group of 50 musicians turned this old bathhouse into a venue for progressive classical music, improvised jazz and world music. The municipal bathhouse was built in 1923. During the war, the Nazis turned it into a Jews-only bathhouse. When the bathhouse closed after the war, it became a bicycle factory. Splendor opened in 2012.

331 MUSEUM AMSTERDAM NOORD

332 BADHUIS JAVAPLEIN

The 5 best places to find
ART IN PUBLIC AREAS

---

336 MURAL 'AAN EEN ROOSJE'
Jacob van Lennepstraat / Nassaukade
West ④

This mural, by the Amsterdam artist Rombout Oomen in 2004, depicted a naked woman. Next to it was the poem 'Aan een roosje' (To a little rose) by Jacob van Lennep. After protests from squeamish neighbours, the woman's pubic hair was pixelated.

337 BANDENBOOT
Oostenburgerdwarsstraat
Oostelijke Eilanden ②

In 1972, the municipality asked Robert Jasper Grootveld to design a climbing frame for kids. The artist built a 'tire boat' made of soft tires, allowing it to 'ride' on the waves. The boat was almost disposed of several years ago. Progressive parties in the city's government, however, managed to prove its cultural and historical value.

338 DE STAM
Frederik Hendrikplantsoen
Westerpark Q ④

Once upon a time, the timber industry dominated this area. Joep van Lieshout was inspired by this history when he created an artwork for this renovated park. The five red, slightly surreal figures in this large sculpture all carry logs ('stam' in Dutch), showing how all layers of society used to work together.

339 SCHUTTERSGALERIJ

Kalverstraat 92
Old Centre ②
+31 (0)20 523 18 22
www.amsterdam
museum.nl

In the 16th and 17th centuries, wealthy Dutchmen commissioned group portraits of themselves. The most famous of these so-called *schutterstukken* (paintings of civic militia men) is Rembrandt's Night Watch in the Rijksmuseum. The Amsterdam Museum exhibits a selection of similar paintings in their Schuttersgalerij, a freely accessible museum alley parallel to Kalverstraat.

340 LA DEMEURE HUMAINE

Westeinde 1
Canal Belt South ③

When the Dutch National Bank moved its headquarters to its current location in Frederiksplein in the sixties, the bank commissioned the Belarusian sculptor Ossip Zadkine to embellish the new building. The result was 'La Demeure Humaine' (the human residence), a 4-metre high bronze statue.

337 BANDENBOOT

The 5 most surprising
WORKS IN THE
MUSEUM QUARTER

---

341 VAN GOGH'S LAST PAINTING

VAN GOGH MUSEUM
Museumplein 6
Museum Q ③
+31 (0)20 570 52 00
www.vangogh
museum.nl

Wheatfield with Crows (1890) was long considered Vincent van Gogh's last painting before he committed suicide. It depicts a dead end, a darkening sky, a harbinger of things to come. Now experts consider *Tree Roots* (1890) a likelier candidate. They say his death explains the irregular, unfinished appearance of the painting. Both works are on display in the museum.

342 JAPANESE TEMPLE GUARDS

RIJKSMUSEUM
Museumstraat 1
Museum Q ③
+31 (0)20 674 70 00
www.rijksmuseum.nl

The Rijksmuseum is known for its many iconic paintings by Rembrandt, Vermeer and Frans Hals. But the museum's vast permanent collection spans centuries of global history. Recently two statues that once guarded the entrance of a 14th-century Japanese temple were added to the Asia galleries. Their purpose was to keep evil out – hence their ferocious looks.

343 HUGO GROTIUS' BOOK CHEST

RIJKSMUSEUM

Museumstraat 1

Museum Q ③

+31 (0)20 674 70 00

www.rijksmuseum.nl

The exceptionally gifted, 17th-century legal scholar Hugo Grotius – or Hugo de Groot – ended up embroiled in a conflict between the civil and religious authorities. He was sentenced to life-long imprisonment as a result, but managed to escape on 22 March 1621. It is believed he did so in the wooden book chest that is on display in the Rijksmuseum.

344 THE KAZIMIR MALEVICH COLLECTION

STEDELIJK MUSEUM

Museumplein 10

Museum Q ③

+31 (0)20 573 29 11

www.stedelijk.nl

The Stedelijk Museum has a large collection of paintings, drawings and sketches by the Russian futurist Kazimir Malevich. The collection was amassed by the Russian writer and art collector Nikolai Khardzhiev, who personally knew many of the Futurists. His collection found its way to Amsterdam in the 1990s.

345 THE BEANERY BY EDWARD KIENHOLZ

STEDELIJK MUSEUM

Museumplein 10

Museum Q ③

+31 (0)20 573 29 11

www.stedelijk.nl

The coolest part of *The Beanery* (1965) by the American artist Edward Kienholz is that you can actually step inside of it. The work is a remake of the artist's favourite bar in Los Angeles. He copied the bottles, posters, the jukebox and even the bar. Everything looks real, except for the people who are all acquaintants of the artist. They have clocks instead of faces.

The 5 best places to enjoy
CLASSICAL MUSIC

———

346 WAALSE KERK
Walenpleintje 159
Old Centre ②
+31 (0)20 623 20 74
www.dewaalsekerk.nl

This Walloon Church was built as a Roman Catholic monastery in 1496. The rise of Protestantism resulted in the ousting of Catholicism from the city. After Amsterdam had dismissed its Catholic government in 1578, the church became a refuge for Walloon protestants and Huguenots who'd fled the Southern Netherlands and France. Concerts are organised here about once a week.

347 ORGELPARK
Gerard Brandt-straat 26
South ⑥
+31 (0)20 515 81 11
www.orgelpark.nl

The wholly renovated Park Church, built in the early 20th century, is now a venue where pipe organ music and live performances in classical, jazz and improvised music are combined. Orgelpark occasionally also shows film and dance performances with organ music.

348 MUZIEKGEBOUW AAN 'T IJ

Piet Heinkade 1
Oostelijke Eilanden ②
+31 (0)20 788 20 00
www.muziekgebouw.nl

The concert hall Muziekgebouw aan 't IJ is the main venue for contemporary classical music. There are two stages, which are both famous for the acoustics and were designed to facilitate a range of music genres. The ground floor has a cafe-restaurant with a large patio from where you can watch the sun set over the River IJ.

349 HET CONCERTGEBOUW

Concertgebouw-plein 10
Museum Q ③
0900 6718345
www.concertgebouw.nl

Since the 1890s, Het Concertgebouw has been the most prominent concert hall for classical music in the country. Over 900 activities are organised here every year. Free lunch concerts are programmed every Wednesday at 12.30 pm, from September to June. The programme is usually announced one week in advance, and includes rehearsals of the Royal Concertgebouw Orchestra, performances by talented young musicians and contemporary music.

350 NEDPHO DOME

Batjanstraat 3
Indische buurt ⑤
+31 (0)20 521 75 00
www.orkest.nl

The Dutch Philharmonic Orchestra uses the renovated, former Gerardus Majella Catholic church in Indische Buurt as its home base, which makes it the only orchestra in the Netherlands to have such a beautiful, well-equipped concert venue all to itself. Concerts are scheduled several times a week.

5 places to see
LIVE MUSIC

---

351 BITTERZOET
Spuistraat 2
Old Centre ②
+31 (0)20 421 23 18
www.bitterzoet.com

Red stained glass windows featuring nudes, an upstairs smoking lounge with comfortable sofas, and a restaurant next door which serves Asian street food. These are just some of the benefits that Bitterzoet has to offer. This intimate venue is known for its R&B and hip-hop parties, but also hosts regular live concerts, featuring a wide range of musical styles, from rock, pop, soul and funk to electro and hip-hop.

352 MELKWEG
Lijnbaansgracht 234-A
Canal Belt South ③
+31 (0)20 531 81 81
www.melkweg.nl

In the early seventies, this former milk factory was converted into a cultural centre, with a music and theatre hall, a tea house and a restaurant. Over the years, Melkweg expanded and now boasts two downstairs concert halls, an exhibition space and restaurant, and an upstairs cinema and theatre. It's also home to the annual 5 Days Off festival for electronic music.

353 PARADISO

Weteringschans 6-8
Canal Belt South ③
+31 (0)20 626 45 21
www.paradiso.nl

This former church was squatted in the sixties and became a 'cosmic relaxation centre'. Paradiso is now one of the most legendary concert venues of Amsterdam, its nickname is 'The pop temple'. The downstairs hall still has a very distinct church feel to it, with stained glass windows and a high ceiling. In addition to being a concert hall, Paradiso is also a night club.

354 AMSTERDAMSE BOSTHEATER

De Duizendmeter-
weg 7
Amstelveen (suburbs)
+31 (0)20 670 02 50
www.bostheater.nl

Come summertime, Amsterdamse Bos is the place to go for plays and concerts in a fairytale open-air setting. The forest serves as a backdrop for the stage, the audience watches from wooden benches, wine in hand. Blankets are supplied on colder evenings. Before the show, have a bite to eat or buy a drink from the food trucks lined up near the entrance.

355 ROODE BIOSCOOP

Haarlemmerplein 7
Haarlemmer Q ①
+31 (0)20 625 75 00
www.roodebioscoop.nl

In the early 20th century the socialist and anarchist Gerhard Rijnders ran this cinema. He was inspired by the ideas of Ferdinand Domela Nieuwenhuis (you'll find his statue opposite the entrance to Westerpark). Now it's a music, theatre and poetry club that's known for its Sunday afternoon performances, or *Roode Zondagen* (red Sundays).

The 5 best places to enjoy
LIVE JAZZ MUSIC

---

356 BIMHUIS
Piet Heinkade 3
Oostelijke Eilanden ②
+31 (0)20 788 21 50
www.bimhuis.nl

Bimhuis has been a leading jazz club since the 1970s. Until they moved to their current location in 2005, the venue was located near the Red Light District. Bimhuis now shares a building with the contemporary music hall Muziekgebouw aan 't IJ. Their concerts feature established artists, young talents and conservatory students.

357 JAZZ CAFÉ ALTO
Korte Leidsedwars-
straat 115
Canal Belt South ③
+31 (0)6 270 70 332
www.jazz-cafe-alto.nl

The atmosphere in Alto is that of an underground jazz club. It opened in 1953 and is one of the oldest jazz cafes in the city, with live jazz and blues shows seven days a week. Doors open every day at 9 pm and close in the wee morning hours.

358 ZAAL 100
De Wittenstraat 100
Westerpark Q ④
+31 (0)20 688 01 27
www.zaal100.nl

'From squatters to guardians of culture', that's how the founders of Zaal 100 once described themselves. In 1984, a group of squatters converted an empty girls' school into a progressive jazz club. The venue became legal in 1992, but stayed true to its roots with its cutting-edge programme.

359 CAFÉ NEL
Amstelveld 12
Canal Belt South ③
+31 (0)20 626 11 99
www.nelamstelveld.nl

Every Monday night, Café Nel is all about jazz. You can have dinner here or just enjoy the music over a drink. The jazz sessions frequently attract musicians who like to climb on the stage themselves as the evening progresses. Musicians who played at Nel in the past included Marcus Miller and Caro Emerald. Concerts are free of charge and start around 9 pm.

360 ON THE ROOF FESTIVAL
AT: BUILDING 'OP ZEEZAND'
Johan van Hasseltweg 39
North ⑦
www.on-the-roof.com

The On the Roof festival takes place on the weekend from June until August. Concerts are organised on a rooftop terrace in Amsterdam North, in an intimate setting with about 100 seats. Discover surprising artists, who don't fit in mainstream genres, who perform everything from jazz to world and classical music.

359 CAFÉ NEL

The 5 smallest
THEATRES

---

361 TORPEDO THEATER
**Sint Pieters-
poortsteeg 33**
Old Centre ②
+31 (0)20 428 49 93
www.torpedotheater.nl

You easily walk past Torpedo Theater, a tiny theatre in a narrow alley in the Red Light District. The building was once used as a puppet theatre. On the programme are talk shows, literary evenings, and performances by singer-songwriters and comedians.

362 BETTY ASFALT COMPLEX
**Nieuwezijds
Voorburgwal 282**
Old Centre ②
+31 (0)20 626 46 95
www.bettyasfalt.nl

The Betty Asfalt Complex is owned by theatre maker, TV writer and comedian Paul Haenen, who's known for his many satirical characters on Dutch television. The theatre is located in a national monument from the early 18th century. The programme offers cabaret and music performances, as well as literary evenings.

363 VEEM HOUSE FOR PERFORMANCE
**Van Diemen-
straat 408-410**
Haarlemmer Q ①
+31 (0)20 626 01 12
www.veem.house

This theatre hosts performances at the interface of performing arts and dance. It's located in the Veem, a building that offers work spaces for small companies, artists and artisans, and has an exhibition space as well. The former warehouse, built in the 19th century to store luxury goods, was squatted in 1981.

364 DE KLEINE KOMEDIE

Amstel 56-58
Waterlooplein Q ②
+31 (0)20 624 05 34
www.dekleine
komedie.nl

This trend-setting cabaret launched the careers of many popular Dutch comedians. The theatre's reputation and intimate setting (503 seats) makes it the most-prized venue in Dutch comedy. Its history dates back to 1786. During WWII, it was used as a bicycle parking. It reopened in its current form in 1948.

365 PODIUM MOZAÏEK

Bos en Lommer-
weg 191
West ④
+31 (0)20 580 03 80
www.podiummozaiek.nl

The former Reformed Pniëlkerk in the Bos en Lommer quarter was converted into a theatre at the beginning of this century. On the programme are world music, cabaret, and theatre and dance performances from the Netherlands and abroad. Theater Café Podium serves dishes from all over the world and has a large patio.

365 PODIUM MOZAÏEK

5 good-to-know
B A N D S
from Amsterdam

---

366 THE EX
www.theex.nl

The Ex is an internationally known underground punk band. The Ex was founded in 1979, its members belonged to the Amsterdam squatting scene. The band lived and played in squatted houses and released many of their albums themselves. Their lyrics are about the squatting scene, the civil wars of Latin America and strikes throughout Europe.

367 BETTIE SERVEERT
www.bettieserveert.com

One of the best-selling records in Concerto Recordstore, which was also recently re-released on vinyl, is *Palomine*. The breakthrough album of Bettie Serveert (Bettie Serves), an indie rock band named after Dutch tennis player Betty Stöve, was originally released in 1992. The band has been going strong since the early nineties and has toured extensively in the United States.

368 WEVAL
weval.bandcamp.com

Merijn Scholte Albers and Harm Coolen first met in film school, but soon they started to make electronic music together. They performed their first live gig in 2013 and their reputation took off from there. You'll hear influences of trip-hop, rock and jazz in their dreamily hypnotic and very danceable tunes.

369 MOKE
www.mokemusic.com

Some people think that Moke's band name is derived from Mokum, a nickname for Amsterdam. That isn't the case, band members say, but Moke is truly an Amsterdam band nevertheless. They play a mixture of indie rock and Britpop. Some of their more popular songs are *Switch* and *Last Tune*. The band is signed to record label Excelsior, which has several Dutch indie bands under contract.

370 MOSS
www.mosstheband.com

Moss is one of the many local bands that used the shelter in Vondel Park as their rehearsal space in their early years. The band's songs are complex. They once had a potential hit song removed from an album. It was too easy, they said. Moss' second album *Never Be Scared/Don't Be a Hero* from 2009 instantly became a Dutch music classic.

The 5 best places for
DEBATE AND LITERATURE

___

371 DE BALIE
**Kleine-Gartman-
plantsoen 10
Canal Belt South** ③
+31 (0)20 553 51 00
www.debalie.nl

The De Balie debating centre in Leidseplein has been a place for thought-
provoking debates on a range of political
and cultural topics and arts projects since
the early 1980s. De Balie also has a small
cinema, a theatre and an informal cafe
and restaurant. English programmes are
occasionally scheduled as well.

372 MEDIAMATIC
**Dijkspark 6
Oostelijke Eilanden** ②
+31 (0)20 638 99 01
www.mediamatic.net

This is a platform for new art and culture
that pays special attention to nature
and biotechnology. Its headquarters –
and greenhouse – are used to connect
people from different backgrounds. They
organise workshops on hydroponics and
the use of mushrooms as biomaterial, as
well as lectures and exhibitions by bio-
artists and designers.

373 PERDU
**Kloveniersburgwal 86
Old Centre** ②
+31 (0)20 627 62 95
www.perdu.nl

Perdu is run by about 40 volunteers and
is all about literature. It's a literary venue
for lectures and debate on literature as
well as a poetry book shop. Perdu is also
a small publishing house.

374 PAKHUIS DE ZWIJGER

Piet Heinkade 179
Oostelijk Eilanden ②
+31 (0)20 624 63 80
www.dezwijger.nl

This former *pakhuis* (warehouse) was built as to store perishables in the thirties. It was squatted after the building had lost its original use. At that time, it was a rehearsal space for musicians such as Herman Brood and Loïs Lane. In 2006, a debating centre opened here, focusing on urban issues and politics, creative or bottom-up initiatives, and innovation.

375 FELIX MERITIS

Keizersgracht 324
Old Centre ②
+31 (0)20 627 94 77
www.felixmeritis.nl

The renowned Felix Meritis cultural centre was founded in 1777 by a society of rich citizens. After the war, the Dutch Communist Party moved in and it became a popular destination for avant-garde musicians and theatre makers. An entrepreneur and philanthropist bought the centre after it closed down in 2014. The centre is scheduled to reopen in 2019, after renovations.

374 PAKHUIS DE ZWIJGER

GEITENBOERDERIJ RIDAMMERHOEVE

30 THINGS TO DO WITH CHILDREN

The 5 best
PLAYGROUNDS

376 BOUWSPEELPLAATS HET LANDJE

Rembrandtpark 1
West ④
+31 (0)20 618 36 04

An adventure playground where generations of kids have romped around since 1972. It's a place where children can build huts, climb trees, pet the animals, enjoy a ride on a pony, where they can learn arts and crafts, how to cook or paddle a canoe. Located on an island, Het Landje is a place where kids between the ages of 6 and 14 can run around freely and get their clothes dirty. Open from Wednesday till Sunday.

377 TUNFUN

Mr. Visserplein 7
Waterlooplein Q ②
+31 (0)20 689 43 00
www.tunfun.nl

Rollerskating, bouncing on trampolines, a ball pit, a football court, and a blow-up survival course: these are just some of the attractions in this huge underground playground. It's located in an old traffic underpass near Waterlooplein and caters to kids of different ages, so young kids won't end up being bowled over by the older, boisterous kids. It's a great place to go on rainy days.

378 HET WOESTE WESTEN

Overbrakerpad 3
Westerpark Q ④
www.woestewesten.nl

A nature playground where you're meant to get your hands and knees dirty. Find frogs, fish and insects, frolic in a stream, pick wildflowers, build a hut, and bake your own bread over a camp fire. Kids are free to explore the different islands. While they're playing, they learn about nature. There's always a caretaker present, but keep an eye on small children near the water.

379 JEUGDLAND

Valentijnkade 131
Watergraafsmeer ⑤
+31 (0)20 463 69 12
www.maakland.nl

Ride in a go-cart, learn how to use a saw and hammer and build your own hut, or bake a pie. At Jeugdland, the possibilities are endless. Even when it's raining there's enough to do indoors, such as table tennis or table football, drawing or playing games. There's also a petting zoo, with a horse called DJ and two donkeys called Kobus and Liesje.

380 AMSTELPARK

Amstelpark 18
South ⑥
+31 (0)20 644 17 44
www.speeltuin-
amstelpark.nl

Amstelpark was built for the 1972 Floriade, an international horticultural exhibition. Besides being a beautifully landscaped park, there's lots to do for children. There is a large playground with swings and slides, a labyrinth, a mini-train, a petting zoo and a mini-golf course. Don't forget to treat yourself and the kids to a big scoop of Italian ice cream from De IJstuin.

The 5 best
MUSEUMS *for* KIDS

381 TASSENMUSEUM HENDRIKJE

Herengracht 573
Canal Belt South ③
+31 (0)20 524 64 52
www.tassenmuseum.nl

It's not the first place you would think of, but Tassenmuseum Hendrikje is a great place for kids. See a tortoise shell purse inlaid with pearl, or modern bags in the shape of a cupcake or a Coca Cola can. Kids can participate in a scavenger hunt, take a special tour or have their own tea party.

382 VERZETSMUSEUM JUNIOR

Plantage Kerklaan 61
Plantage Q ②
+31 (0)20 620 25 35
www.verzets
museum.org

In the resistance museum, kids learn more about WWII through the stories of four ten-year olds: Nelly, Henk, Eva and Jan. Their experiences as a Jewish girl, or as the son of a Dutch resistance hero, lead you through the war, bringing history to life and making it more tangible. It's a fantastic interactive experience.

383 NEMO SCIENCE CENTRE

Oosterdok 2
Old Centre ②
+31 (0)20 531 32 33
www.e-nemo.nl

You can't miss the giant green hull of NEMO next to Central Station. It's a modern 4-storey museum catering to kids, but it's educational for adults as well. 'Find out for yourself how the world works' is their motto. Learn why your hair stands on end in winter, or to build your own dam.

384 TROPENMUSEUM JUNIOR

Linnaeusstraat 2
Oosterpark Q ⑤
+31 (0)88 004 28 40
www.tropenmuseum
junior.nl

When the Tropenmuseum Junior opened in 1975, the problem was that there were too many visitors. The market vendors and visitors of Dappermarkt liked to drop off their little tots here, so better give these shrieking kids something to do. This award-winning museum hosts interactive exhibitions to experience different cultures from around the world.

385 STEDELIJK MUSEUM / FAMILY LAB

Museumplein 10
Museum Q ③
+31 (0)20 573 29 11
www.stedelijk.nl/
educatie/families

Make your own Willem de Kooning painting or a Matisse cut-out in the Familylab. There are scavenger hunts and special family (audio) tours featuring the museum's modern art highlights with several hands-on assignments to complete. On Sunday afternoons there are workshops by artists and designers (usually in Dutch).

381 TASSENMUSEUM HENDRIKJE

The 5 nicest places for
OUTDOOR FUN

386 KINDERBOERDERIJ WESTERPARK

Overbrakerpad 10
Westerpark Q ④
+31 (0)20 682 21 93
www.kinderboerderij
westerpark.nl

This petting zoo has lots of different goats, sheep, ponies, and a cow called Teuke. There are also smaller animals to pet, including rabbits and guinea pigs. Besides animals, there's a great playground. It makes for a nice stop when walking through the Westerpark. Sit down and enjoy a coffee or lemonade on the terrace.

387 GEITENBOERDERIJ RIDAMMERHOEVE

Nieuwe Meerlaan 4
Amsterdamse Bos /
Amstelveen
+31 (0)20 645 50 34
www.geitenboerderij.nl

Goats galore! At this working farm, white dairy goats roam around big barns. They are curious animals and can be petted. You can even feed the little ones a bottle of milk. There's a shop where they sell goat's milk products, and a nice self-service restaurant.

388 ARTIS

Plantage Kerk-
laan 38-40
Plantage Q ②
0900 2784796
www.artis.nl

This old city zoo has put a lot of work into turning its outdated confined cages into natural and spacious environments. Visit the bird and monkey houses where the tiniest monkeys jump around your head in the same space where large green iguanas roam around freely and bats hang from the ceiling.

389 KINDERBOERDERIJ DE UYLENBURG

Staalmeesters-
laan 420
New-West ④
+31 (0)20 618 52 35
*www.kinderboerderij-
uylenburg.nl*

This fun little petting zoo is located in the outer most corner of Rembrandt Park, close to the Ramada Apollo Hotel. They have goats, pigs, horses and numerous small animals such as rabbits, chicken and turkeys. You can buy animal feed for just 50 cents and feed the critters. There's also a small playground and a nice terrace to enjoy a coffee or a chocolate milk.

390 FUN FOREST

Bosbaanweg 3
Amsterdamse Bos /
Amstelveen
+31 (0)88 369 70 00
www.funforest.nl

Soar through the treetops on a zip wire, climb up ladders and make your way across flimsy rope ladders. There are nine different climbing and survival courses in this tree park, suitable for kids 4 years and up. The three-hour climbing experience is fun for adults as well, although some courses are for kids only.

390 FUN FOREST

5 child-friendly
CAFES/RESTAURANTS

391 KANARIE CLUB

Bellamyplein 51
West ④
+31 (0)20 218 17 75
www.kanarieclub.nl

Kanarie Club is located at one end of De Hallen, an old tram depot that was converted into several restaurants, food stalls, a hotel, a cinema, a library, galleries and shops. Kanarie Club has a nice spacious sunny terrace, and a special menu for kids, with toasties, a mini-burger and dame blanche for dessert. Open all day.

392 BOERDERIJ MEERZICHT

Koenenkade 56
Amsterdamse Bos /
Amstelveen
+31 (0)20 679 27 44
www.boerderij
meerzicht.nl

This farm on the edge of Amsterdamse Bos is a popular spot for a rest. This self-service restaurant mainly serves pancakes, but also has sandwiches. The real draw is the large terrace. Parents can relax while their children run around and visit the playground or the petting zoo with spotted deer and peacocks.

393 VONDELTUIN

Vondelpark 7
South ⑥
+31 (0)6 275 65 576
www.devondeltuin.nl

At the southern end of Vondelpark lies a secluded garden. Vondeltuin (Vondel garden) is the perfect place to take your kids and have a drink while they play. Because the terrace is fenced off, the kids can gallivant safely. The cafe serves a good selection of snacks and simple main courses. Closed in winter.

394 LUNCHROOM LASTIG

Christiaan
Huygensplein 33
Watergraafsmeer ⑤
+31 (0)20 35 41 676
*www.lunchroom
lastig.nl*

Indonesian *nasi kuning* and Dutch *wentelteefjes* (french toast) on one and the same menu: life doesn't get any better than this. Lunchroom Lastig (*lastig* is Dutch for difficult) serves breakfast and lunch with normal Dutch fare as well as Indonesian options. Lastig feels like a neighbourhood living room, but one with a special treat: a 40-square-metre game room.

395 PACIFIC PARC

Polonceaukade 23
Westerpark Q ④
+31 (0)20 488 77 78
www.pacificparc.nl

Pacific Parc is located at the far end of the former gasworks in Westerpark. It has a large sunny terrace. Indoors you will find a roaring fire in the fireplace on chillier days. A nice, spacious place for a coffee or lunch, with room for kids to run around. In the evenings it's a good place for a drink and some dancing.

The 5 best
SHOPS for KIDS

396 GOOCHEM SPEELGOED

Eerste Constantijn
Huygensstraat 80
West ④
+31 (0)20 612 47 04
www.goochem.nl

This family-owned store has been manu-facturing toys from natural materials since the early eighties, initially selling them from their own workshop. They soon moved to a larger store and now sell over 75 different brands. Do check out their beautifully crafted wooden toys and animals.

397 DE KINDERBOEK-WINKEL

Rozengracht 34
De Jordaan ①
+31 (0)20 622 47 61
www.kinderboek
winkel.nl

Tow-Truck Pluck's little red tow-truck is parked outside of this store, which Rietje Nivard opened in 1975. De Kinderboek-winkel sells classics like *The Very Hungry Caterpillar* (Rupsje Nooitgenoeg) and Dick Bruna's *Nijntje* (Miffy) as well as audiobooks and young adult fiction. There's a second store at Nieuwezijds Voorburgwal 344.

398 KNUFFELS

Sint Antoniebree-straat 51-A
Waterlooplein Q ②
+31 (0)20 427 38 62
www.pluche.nl

Knuffels (Dutch for cuddly toys) is located in a former entrance to the metro station. Upstairs you'll find animals from all the continents, downstairs is a clog shop. Owner Bruno Jonker makes wooden shoes to order in different colours and sizes.

399 MECHANISCH SPEELGOED

Westerstraat 67
De Jordaan ①
+31 (0)20 638 16 80

Mechanisch Speelgoed sells authentic toys, such as wooden building buckets, puppets in all sizes, tin soldiers, stuffed animals and balls, avoiding all the popular film and cartoon characters and the loud, battery-powered stuff. When stepping across the threshold, it's as if you're travelling back in time several decades.

400 DE ZAAILING

Ruysdaelstraat 21-23
Museum Q ③
+31 (0)20 679 38 17
www.zaailing.nl

De Zaailing is a light and spacious store, located on a quiet street tucked in between the Rijksmuseum and De Pijp, that appeals to people who prefer natural products. They sell anthroposophical books for children and grown-ups, wooden toys, music boxes, Trousellier's magical lamps, and clothes for all ages.

396 GOOCHEM SPEELGOED

The 5 best

CHILDREN'S THEATRES

---

401 JEUGDTHEATER DE KRAKELING

Nieuwe
Passeerdersstraat 1
Canal Belt South ③
+31 (0)20 624 51 23
www.krakeling.nl

This red brick Dutch Renaissance building used to be a gymnastics room, but in the late seventies it was converted into a youth theatre. De Krakeling plays · mime and music, puppet theatre and dance theatre. The stage is level with the audience seats, creating an intimate atmosphere. They cater to kids all ages.

402 OOSTBLOK

Sajetplein 39
Oosterpark Q ⑤
+31 (0)20 665 45 68
www.oostblok.nl

Oostblok is a popular children's theatre in East. Once a month, toddlers can enjoy theatre on Wednesday mornings. On Sundays, there are shows for children of different ages, starting with a theatrical adventure for 1-year olds. They also offer theatre courses for 6 to 12-year olds.

403 AMSTERDAM MARIONETTE THEATRE

Nieuwe Jonkerstraat 8
Old Centre ②
+31 (0)20 620 80 27
www.marionetten
theater.nl

In this former ship's smithy, the tradition of European classical puppet theatre is kept alive. Wooden puppets in white wigs and velvet costumes star in an opera, singing Mozart's Magic Flute or Offenbach's Castle in the Air. Very enjoyable, even if you don't speak Dutch.

404 SO WHAT CHILDREN CONCERTS
AT: DE DUIF
Prinsengracht 756
Canal Belt South ③
www.sowhat
kinderconcerten.nl

Once a month four musicians play classical music, jazz and playful sounds for kids from the age of two in a church called De Duif. Concerts last an hour, and the atmosphere is very informal. Kids are encouraged to join in by clapping, dancing and singing, and are even invited to join the musicians on stage with their own instruments.

405 MUZIEKGEBOUW AAN 'T IJ – FOR KIDS
Piet Heinkade 1
Oostelijke Eilanden ②
+31 (0)20 788 20 00
www.muziekgebouw.nl/
jeugd

On Wednesday and Sunday afternoons, kids can play with sound installations at Muziekgebouw aan 't IJ, teaching them how to make sounds and how to compose music. On children's afternoons in 't Muziekgebouw, there are concerts for different ages: theatrical shows for the little ones and jazz performances for kids 10 and up.

402 OOSTBLOK

HOUSEBOAT MS LUCTOR

25 PLACES TO SLEEP

The 5 best
DESIGN HOTELS

406 ART'OTEL

Prins Hendrikkade 33
Old Centre ②
+31 (0)20 719 7200
www.artotel
amsterdam.com

Conveniently located near Amsterdam's Central Station in a bustling, scruffy tourist area. Inside, the recently opened Art'otel is all sleek style and design. The 107 rooms are decorated in all shades of grey, with slashes of bright colour. Downstairs, the 5&33 bar and restaurant serves early breakfasts and excellent cocktails.

407 KAMER 01

Singel 416
Canal Belt South ③
+31 (0)6 547 76 151
www.kamer01.
amsterdam

There is a lavishly decorated room in blue, red or green on each of the three floors of this 16th-century canal house. The rooms have en-suite marble bathrooms and seating area. A five-course champagne breakfast is served on the first floor. The rooftop terrace is the ideal place to enjoy a pre-dinner drink.

408 ANDAZ HOTEL

Prinsengracht 587
Canal Belt South ③
+31 (0)20 523 12 34
www.amsterdam
prinsengracht.
andaz.hyatt.com

The interior of this former quiet public library is an explosion of colour, shapes and bright lights. The designer Marcel Wanders created the design scheme for this five-star hotel that includes references to the Golden Age and toilets decorated with modern Delft Blue tiles.

409 LLOYD HOTEL

Oostelijke
Handelskade 34
Oostelijke Eilanden ②
+31 (0)20 561 36 07
www.lloydhotel.com

Built in the twenties as accommodation for migrants on their way to America this building was subsequently used as a prison before being turned into a hotel. There are 117 rooms designed by artists ranging from 1 to 5 star quality. The restaurant and lounge area opens onto a large sunny terrace. Lloyd Hotel also has a library of about 2000 art books.

410 VOLKSHOTEL

Wibautstraat 150
Oosterpark Q ⑤
+31 (0)20 261 2100
www.volkshotel.nl

The old newspaper buildings on the Wibautstraat have all found a new purpose. In 2014, the Volkshotel opened in the former *Volkskrant* building, offering small, standard rooms as well as a bicycle-themed suite and a Johnny Jukebox room for music lovers. There's a restaurant and club on the top floor (Canvas) with spectacular views of the city, as well as a rooftop hot tub and sauna.

408 ANDAZ HOTEL

The 5 most
UNUSUAL PLACES TO SLEEP

---

411 FARALDA NDSM CRANE HOTEL

NDSM-Plein 78
North ⑦
+31 (0)20 760 61 61
www.faralda.com

Sleeping in this monumental dockside crane is not for the faint of heart as the three suites are 50 metres above the city. There's a rooftop pool and thrill-seekers can even bungee jump from the crane. The rooms are lavishly decorated, with a golden ceiling, a stuffed peacock next to the bed and a blue and purple love nest.

412 HOTEL NOT HOTEL

Piri Reisplein 34
West ④
+31 (0)20 820 45 38
www.hotelnothotel.com

In this hotel in the western part of town, a room isn't just a room, but an art installation. A group of young designers created intimate sleeping spaces. You can sleep inside an old tram car, in a crow's nest, or behind a secret book case. While the rooms are small, there are enough nooks and crannies in the hotel to relax in.

413 FLORES & PUCK

Rietwijkerstraat 51
South ⑥
+31 (0)6 445 31 522
www.amsterdam
bedandbreakfast.org

Astrid and her daughter Sammy run this bed and breakfast. The cottage at the end of their garden has its own entrance and a sunny terrace where, weather permitting, breakfast is served every morning. Astrid always has good tips for exploring Amsterdam. You can also rent a bike.

414 CAKE UNDER MY PILLOW

Eerste Jacob van
Campenstraat 66–2
De Pijp ③
+31 (0)20 751 09 36
www.cakeunder
mypillow.com

A bed and breakfast located above the famous cake shop 'De taart van mijn tante' (co-owner Siemon de Jong is the host of a kids talk show on TV). Downstairs the cakes are luscious and extravagant, while the upstairs b&b is tastefully decorated and offers rooms with private or shared bathrooms, and has a communal kitchen and living room.

415 AMSTERDAM COUNTRY COTTAGE

Durgerdammer-
gouw 51
North ⑦
+31 (0)6 294 36 357
www.amsterdam
countrycottage.nl

A two-floor country cottage in the middle of a bird sanctuary, with its own dock and terrace with a barbecue. It's a great place to enjoy nature and only a stone's throw from the city, although it might be difficult to get to without a car. Compared to hotel prices in the city, the cottage is great value for money.

411 FARALDA NDSM CRANE HOTEL

5

HOTELS
with HISTORY

416 AMRATH HOTEL

Prins Hendrik-
kade 108
Old Centre ②
+31 (0)20 552 00 00
www.amrath
amsterdam.com

Het Scheepvaarthuis (the Shipping House) is one of the finest examples of the Amsterdam School architecture. It was built in 1916 as a modern office building for six shipping companies, teeming with references to Holland's rich shipping history. Lavishly decorated, the Shipping House is a feast for the eyes. The building was restored and reopened as a five star hotel in 2007.

417 DE WINDKETEL

Watertorenplein 8-C
Westerpark Q ④
www.windketel.nl

The Windketel is the smallest building on the site of the former municipal gas and waterworks. The small octagonal brick tower, which was built in the late 19th century, is located in a quiet car-free square, somewhat overshadowed by the apartment buildings of an eco-friendly neighbourhood and a large white water tower. Amazingly, this tiny tower is now a three-storey luxury apartment for two, furnished with Dutch design. It is run by a cooperative of neighbours.

417 **DE WINDKETEL**

418 **HILTON AMSTERDAM**

Apollolaan 138
South ⑥
+31 (0)20 710 60 00
www3.hilton.com

John Lennon and Yoko Ono held their famous bed-in for peace here in 1969. On a less positive note, this is also the building singer Herman Brood jumped from to end his life in 2001. When the Hilton Amsterdam opened its doors in 1962, it was the first international chain hotel in the Netherlands. Its v-shape was designed by Dutch architect Hugh Maaskant.

419 **OP HET ALTAAR**

Amstel 98
Old Centre ②
www.ophetaltaar.nl

Sleeping on an altar? It's possible in this church which is tucked away behind Rembrandtplein. In the wake of the Reformation (16th century) clandestine churches popped up in Amsterdam where repressed Catholics could still practice their faith. This 18th-century church looks just like a normal home from the outside. Inside, though, you will discover a luxury apartment, with a bed on the altar.

420 **DOELEN HOTEL**

Nieuwe Doelen-
straat 26
Old Centre ②
+31 (0)20 795 60 88
www.nh-hotels.nl/
hotel/nh-amsterdam-
doelen

This large neo-Renaissance hotel building dates from the late 1900s. Amsterdam's first tour boat departed from here in 1909. It was also where the Beatles stayed when they visited Amsterdam in 1964. Long before that, it was called Kloveniersdoelen or the civic guard's hall. Rembrandt's famous painting The Night Watch used to hang here. NH Doelen is now a 4-star hotel.

The 5 most
ECO-FRIENDLY
PLACES TO SLEEP

---

421 CAMPING AMSTERDAMSE BOS

Kleine Noorddijk 1
Amstelveen (suburbs)
+31 (0)20 641 68 68
www.camping
amsterdamsebos.nl

What could be more eco-friendly than sleeping on a campsite? You can bring your own tent, but also sleep in one of the chalets, cottages or eco-lodges. The eco-lodges are dome-shaped wooden structures, with optional heating and (bunk) beds, sleeping 2 to 4. A basic affair, but more comfortable than sleeping in a tent. There's a communal kitchen and dining area on the campsite.

422 BICYCLE HOTEL

Van Ostadestraat 123
De Pijp ③
+31 (0)20 679 34 52
www.bicyclehotel.com

The Bicycle Hotel is located in a quiet part of the vibrant De Pijp. True to their name, the hotel encourages its guests to use bikes, but the hotel is sustainable in other ways too. Paper and glass are recycled, the owners prefer environmentally-friendly cleaning products and sustainable energy is generated by the solar panels on the green roof. Rooms are simple, clean and affordable. Mornings start with a buffet breakfast.

423 HOTEL V

Weteringschans 136
Canal Belt South ③
+31 (0)20 662 32 33
www.hotelv
frederiksplein.nl

A three-star design hotel located on the fringe of De Pijp. The hotel has a distinctly glamorous feel, with a large crescent-shaped leather sofa around an open fireplace in the lobby. But luxury can be environmentally-friendly as well. Hotel V received a golden green key award for sustainability. The rooms are decorated in a modern, sleek style and vary in size and price.

424 CONSCIOUS HOTEL VONDELPARK

Overtoom 519
West ④
+31 (0)20 820 33 33
www.conscious
hotels.com/
hotelsVondelpark

Desks made out of recycled plastic, a living plant wall, renewable energy and water-saving shower heads. The Conscious Hotel Vondelpark is greener than green. They sell eco-products such as reusable water bottles in their shop, host 'no-waste' dinners, and source their food from local and organic growers. The rooms are modern, with brightly-coloured wallpaper featuring photos of forests, flowers or bamboo behind comfortable beds.

425 ECOMAMA

Valkenburger-
straat 124
Waterlooplein Q ②
+31 (0)20 770 95 29
www.ecomama
hotel.com

A boutique hostel with an industrial interior filled with recycled furniture, including secondhand sofas and a reception desk made of old books. This hostel combines the cosiness of backpackers and bunk beds, with the luxury and service of a hotel. Ecomama has a water saving system, an eco-friendly heating system, and mattresses made from natural, sustainable materials.

RUNNING AROUND
USE the
walkie to
talkie
HOLLA US!

The 5 best places to sleep
ON THE WATER

426 TASMANIA

Houthavens
Westerpark Q ④
www.airbnb.com

A houseboat that looks like a yacht
thanks to its sleek, modern design. It was
especially built for the owners Sonja and
Michiel, who rent out the studio in the
bow through Airbnb (look for 'Tasmania').
The studio has round portholes and
a skylight for gazing out at the stars.
The studio has a private entrance and
deck. Tasmania is located in a quiet
part of Amsterdam.

427 SWEETS HOTEL

VARIOUS LOCATIONS

www.sweetshotel.
amsterdam

If the best way to experience Amsterdam
is from the water, then SWEETS hotel has
bagged the greatest locations for you to
do this. They have hotel rooms in thirty
different bridge houses across the city.
Before the bridges were automated, these
structures were home to the city's bridge
keepers. They've now been turned into
stylish rooms for two.

428 BLUE WAVE HOUSEBOAT

Da Costakade 342
West ④
+31 (0)20 427 89 68
www.bluewave
houseboat.com

The Blue Wave Houseboat is easy to recognise because of its undulating shape and is moored in a quiet residential area, within walking distance of the Jordaan and Ten Kate market. Hans and Elisabeth have lived here for years, and it still feels as if you're visiting friends when you step inside. Watch the geese swim by from the outside deck, or play a little guitar or piano inside.

429 HOUSEBOAT MS LUCTOR

Westerdok 103
Westelijke Eilanden ①
+31 (0)6 226 89 506
www.boat
bedandbreakfast.nl

MS Luctor is a Dutch sailing barge built in 1913. Many of the original features, such as a big wooden steering wheel, have been retained. It was converted into a stylish three-room apartment that makes for a romantic getaway. The ship is moored in an old and quiet residential neighbourhood of Amsterdam called the Westelijke Eilanden. You can use the two bikes or even the Canadian canoe to explore the area.

430 HOUSEBOAT VOLLE MAAN (FULL MOON)

Realengracht 9
Westelijke Eilanden ①
+31 (0)6 224 18 331
www.houseboat
bedandbreakfast.com

Sleep in the rear of a historical ship in an Amsterdam neighbourhood that still has a 17th-century feel to it. Your hosts Pim and Maartje will go out of their way to make their guests feel comfortable. You have your own private entrance and terrace and breakfast is dropped off on your doorstep in a basket.

AMSTERDAMSE BOS

30 WEEKEND ACTIVITIES

———

The 5 best
CYCLING ROUTES

---

431 DURGERDAM AND WATERLAND
(suburbs)

Behind Central Station, take the ferry to Amsterdam North and head northeastwards. Cycle past dike houses on Nieuwendammerdijk and Schelling-wouderdijk, all the way to Durgerdam, a charming fisherman's village. Just a short distance from Durgerdam is Waterland, a large nature reserve with lots of birds. You can return via Schellingwouderbrug and enter the city from the East side, cycling back across Oostelijke Eilanden.

432 OUDERKERK AAN DE AMSTEL
(suburbs)

What could be lovelier than cycling along a river? Just follow the Amstel eastwards and out of the city. You'll eventually reach Ouderkerk a/d Amstel, where you can have a coffee with apple pie or an ice-cream in the old harbour. On your way, you'll pass Amstel Park, a windmill and some amazing mansions. Bike back or take the ferry across the river to give the other shore a try.

433 **AMSTERDAMSE BOS**
Amstelveen (suburbs)

Amsterdamse Bos (a 30-minute cycle ride south from Central Station) was built in the 1930s to provide work for the unemployed. Between 1934 and 1940, 20.000 people worked here. The park was supposed to become the ideal mix of nature and recreation. There are playgrounds, petting zoos, swimming pools, sports fields and a rowing course, as well as large patches of forest, marshes and grasslands.

434 **LANGE BRETTEN**
(suburbs)

Along the train tracks and the road to Haarlem (Haarlemmerweg) lies a small stretch of wilderness called *Lange Bretten*. It's a popular route towards Spaarnwoude and Haarlem. You'll see lots of wildlife in the reeds and bushes including birds, rabbits and weasels. In the summertime, the blackberries produce abundant fruit and near Spaarnwoude, there are lots of places to swim.

435 **RONDE HOEP**
(suburbs)

A favourite trail with racing cyclists, the *Ronde Hoep* route will take you through the polders. It's close to Amsterdam, but intuitively the city feels miles away. You'll swing through tiny farming villages, but mostly you'll see lush green fields as far as the eyes can see, with cows grazing and storks looking for frogs. The whole loop is 17 kilometers. Start from Ouderkerk a/d Amstel.

5

PARKS

you shouldn't miss

---

436 PARK FRANKENDAEL
Watergraafsmeer ⑤
www.park-
frankendael.nl

Frankendael House used to be a country estate for wealthy Amsterdammers and is now a restaurant. The park was opened to the public, but retained its distinguished look and feel. Strolling through this park, you'll feel as if you've travelled back in time to an 18th-century country estate.

437 VLIEGENBOS
North ⑦
www.vliegenbos.info

Vliegenbos in Amsterdam looks anything but excessively landscaped. Its lush trees and bushes have a charm that disappeared from most of the heavily managed parks in the city centre. It was built in 1912 on the initiative of the social democratic city councillor Willem Vliegen, who wanted to create a space in the city where labourers could enjoy nature.

438 SARPHATI PARK

De Pijp ③

Bridges, winding paths and lavishly overgrown: this scenic 19th-century park is the younger brother of the Vondelpark, the first Dutch park to be built in the English landscape garden style. Sarphati Park offers a welcome escape from the hustle and bustle of De Pijp. Locals can also donate or swap seeds, sprouts and plants at the ecological recycling agency in the park.

439 FLEVOPARK

Indische Buurt ⑤
www.flevopark.nl

Vast and quiet Flevopark is located to the east of Indische Buurt. Because of the nearby lake, Het Nieuwe Diep, many birds and other animals find their way to the park. Plans for a scenic area in the eastern part of the city were made in the early twentieth century by Jac P. Thijsse (1865-1945), the Netherlands' best known biologist and conservationist.

440 WERTHEIMPARK

Plantage Q ②

Tiny Wertheimpark in the former Jewish neighbourhood is the only park in the old city centre. It's named after the Jewish entrepreneur and philanthropist Abraham Carel Wertheim, who lived in the 19th century. The name was temporarily changed during WWII, when all references to the royal family or Jews in street names were changed.

The 5 best sights
OUTSIDE AMSTERDAM

---

441 COBRA MUSEUM FOR MODERN ART

Sandbergplein 1
Amstelveen (suburbs)
+31 (0)20 547 50 50
www.cobra-museum.nl

The Cobra Museum has a large collection of works by the post-war CoBrA movement, including such artists as Karel Appel, Corneille, Pierre Alechinsky, Asger Jorn and Carl-Henning Pedersen. The Japanese-Dutch-American sculptor Shinkichi Tajiri designed an enclosed Japanese Zen garden for the museum. The museum is located in Amstelveen, which is about 40 minutes from Central Station.

442 TEYLERS MUSEUM

Spaarne 16
Haarlem (suburbs)
+31 (0)23 516 09 60
www.teylersmuseum.nl

Founded in 1778, Teylers is the Netherlands' oldest museum. This pleasantly old-fashioned art and science museum still has old wooden cabinets full of fossils and minerals, as well as period rooms full of paintings. There's also a modern extension where they host temporary exhibitions. Teylers is a good excuse to visit Haarlem, which is only 15 minutes away by train.

443 BUITENPLAATS BEECKESTIJN

Rijksweg 134
Velsen-Zuid (suburbs)
+31 (0)25 552 28 77
*www.buitenplaats
beeckestijn.nl*

Rich Amsterdammers would flee the crowded, smelly city and spend summers in their country houses. At Buitenplaats Beeckestijn you can see what such a summer house would have looked like. Its history dates back to the 16th century, serving as a home to several Amsterdam mayors. Visit the main house and marvel at the old furniture and family portraits or take a leisurely stroll through the romantic English garden or the geometrical French garden.

444 HEMBRUG

Zaandam (suburbs)
*www.hembrug
terrein.com*

For the past 150 years, Hembrug was securely fenced off as weapons, bullets, grenades and at one time even poisonous gases were produced here. In 2003, the last munitions factory shut its doors. Now it's fastly becoming the must-visit site of Zaandam, with resident artists, design studios, shops, museums, cool restaurants and a fabulous forest, which was originally planted to protect Zaandam from explosions.

445 MARKEN

This old fisherman's village with its typical green wooden houses is situated on a peninsula in Markermeer Lake, to the north of Amsterdam. You can easily get to it by bus (the 315 from Central Station), but it's even nicer to bike there. There's a museum and a famous souvenir shop, but the village itself and the views on the lake are the real attraction.

The 5 most essential
SUMMER FESTIVALS

---

446 PITCH FESTIVAL
Westergasfabriek area
Westerpark Q ④
www.pitchfestival.nl

A two-day summer festival for new electronic music that takes place in tents and on different sites of the old gasworks *(Westergasfabriek)*. Unlike other electronic music festivals, Pitch has a very broad definition of what electronic music is and may programme world music and pop music alongside house and techno.

447 DEKMANTEL FESTIVAL
Amsterdamse Bos
Amstelveen (suburbs)
www.dekmantel
festival.com

This four-day dance festival in early August has become one of the biggest dance festivals in the city. The line-up always holds some special surprises. You can visit venues all over town, from clubs to concert halls. But Amsterdamse Bos is where the magic really happens: dance till morning in natural surroundings.

448 ROLLENDE KEUKENS
Westergasfabriek area
Westerpark Q ④
www.rollende
keukens.nl

Amsterdam's one and only food truck festival. In May, Westerpark is invaded by a hundred cars, mopeds, trucks and vans of all sizes selling all types of street food. When the weather is nice, it's an immensely popular outing, so be prepared to wait in line for your food.

449 LANDJUWEEL FESTIVAL

Ruigoord 76
Ruigoord (suburbs)
www.ruigoord.nl

Landjuweel is a multicultural festival held at the end of August at cultural freehaven Ruigoord. Think free-spirited, happy people enjoying music, theatre, poetry and dance. Ruigoord is a village that was squatted in the 1970s and has been taken over by artists. The inhabitants host regular events, organising shows and workshops in the old church.

450 PLUK DE NACHT

Westerdoksdijk 705-C
Westelijke Eilanden ①
www.plukdenacht.nl

In 2003, a group of film-loving friends got together and started this open-air cinema festival in Amsterdam. The concept: free movies, beach chairs and a fantastic view across the River IJ proved a hit. On some nights, crowds of people actually queue to get in, with some even taking a short cut through the cold water. The festival is held every year in August.

The 5 best
SIGHTSEEING TRIPS
by public transport

---

451 NDSM FERRY
Central Station
Old Centre ②
www.gvb.nl

The ferry link between the northern NDSM dockyard and Amsterdam Central Station gives you a free sightseeing tour in 15 minutes. En route you'll see modern architecture, some old warehouses, and even a Russian submarine from the 1950s. Wind blowing in your hair, boats passing by: what a way to unwind.

452 TRAM 2
Central Station
Old Centre ②
www.gvb.nl

National Geographic listed tram line 2 as one of the best public transport rides in the world. The line departs from Central Station and ends at Oudenaardeplantsoen in New-West. On your way you'll pass Dam square, the Flower Market, Leidseplein, the Rijksmuseum and Vondelpark.

453 TRAM 24
Central Station
Old Centre ②
www.gvb.nl

Tram 24 will take you from the north to the south of the city. The terminus is at VU hospital. Along the way, go shopping in De Pijp, pop into a museum in Museumplein, marvel at the grandeur of De Lairessestraat, see where the 1928 Olympics were held, and end your day in a nice restaurant in Stadionplein.

454 **BUS 22**

Central Station
Old Centre ②
www.gvb.nl

Bus line 22 connects two vibrant areas in the east and west of the city. It departs from Zaanstraat in the western Spaarndammerbuurt passing by Haarlemmerplein, continuing its way along the River IJ, towards Amsterdam's Central Station. From there it leaves for the Plantage quarter, Muiderpoort train station and Javaplein in the Indische Buurt. Its terminus is Th.K. van Lohuizenlaan.

455 **TRAIN TO OVERVEEN**

Central Station
Old Centre ②
www.gvb.nl

The track to Haarlem was the first ever built in the Netherlands. Just past Haarlem lies charming Overveen train station, which was built in 1881. From here it's a short walk to the dunes of the Zuid-Kennemerland national reserve. Walk another 5 kilometres and you'll find yourself in a bathing resort called Zandvoort aan Zee. From here, you can take the train back to Amsterdam.

451 NDSM FERRY

The 5 nicest
AMSTERDAM BEACHES

---

456 **SLOTERPLAS**
West ④

Amsterdam's western garden cities were built using lots of local sand. The sand pit was turned into Sloterplas. There are several good swimming spots around this big lake but if you prefer a real beach, there's one next to Hotel Buiten (Th. J. Lammerslaan 3).

457 **STRAND ZUID**
Europaplein 22
South ⑥
+31 (0)20 639 25 89
www.zuid-pool.nl

A strange location for a beach, but Strand Zuid is next to the RAI convention centre. It's the perfect place to lounge, lazily sip a cocktail or have dinner on the terrace. Most of all it's a place to see and be seen. This city beach has a chique upper class feel to it. You can't actually swim here, but there are showers for cooling off.

458 STRAND WEST

Stavangerweg 900
Westelijke Eilanden ①
+31 (0)20 682 63 10
www.strand-west.nl

This 20.000-square-metre beach is located in Houthavens, a former wood harbour that is currently being redeveloped. Quite a few students live in this area, and Strand West is a popular hangout for them. Here you can lounge in hammocks, eat tapas, sip cocktails or play beach volleyball.

459 ZANDVOORT AAN ZEE

VVV OFFICE:
Bakkerstraat 2-B
Zandvoort aan Zee
(suburbs)
+31 (0)23 571 79 47
www.vvvzandvoort.nl

Zandvoort aan Zee, a popular beach town that attracts a lot of tourists in summer, is only a 30-minute train journey from Amsterdam. It's better to visit in spring or autumn when you'll have more of the beach to yourself. There are many cafes and restaurants on the shorefront from where you can watch the sun set in the sea. Most of them are open all year through.

460 IJMUIDEN AAN ZEE

VVV OFFICE:
Dudokplein 16
IJmuiden aan zee
(suburbs)
+31 (0)20 702 60 00
www.vvvijmuiden
aanzee.nl

IJmuiden aan Zee has one of the widest beaches. The town itself is really down to earth compared with Zandvoort and upper class Bloemendaal, and less crowded too. Maybe it has something to do with those big Tata Steel factory pipes looming in the background. The beach is popular with wind and kitesurfers, and bird-watchers like to congregate on the pier.

HET LIEVERDJE

40 RANDOM FACTS AND URBAN DETAILS

5 places marked by
PROVO

461 HET LIEVERDJE
Spui
Old Centre ②

In 1960, a tobacco trader donated this bronze little boy with the cheeky face to the city. In the mid-sixties, the artist and 'anti-smoke magician' Robert Jasper Grootveld held his happenings here, protesting against the tobacco industry and the power of industry. He and his followers chanted and danced around the statue, occasionally setting it on fire. It's still a popular place for protests.

462 K-TEMPEL
Korte Leidse
Dwarsstraat
Canal Belt South ③

Robert Jasper Grootveld started his anti-smoke happenings in a 'tempel' near Leidseplein. In a time when smoking was still accepted as normal, Grootveld painted big K's (K for the Dutch word for cancer) on cigarette commercials. In his temple, he burnt cigarettes on an altar creating a lot of smoke. His services for 'conscious nicotinists' drew a lot of attention, but after a month, the temple went up in flames.

463 APOLLO BIOSCOOP

Haarlemmerdijk 82
Haarlemmer Q ①

This old cinema became a provo meeting place. The neighbourhood was not too happy about the arrival of these 'long-haired lazy layabouts'. They organised meetings and people regularly stayed the night. A riot took place in 1967 when a group of marines came looking for provos to beat up. The police tried to intervene, but the situation ultimately got out of hand. The cinema was instantly closed. It's now a budget hotel.

464 THE HOUSE OF ROEL VAN DUIJN AND ROB STOLK

Karthuizersstraat 14
De Jordaan ①

Provo became a real movement when Roel van Duijn gave it the name provo in May 1965. He met Rob Stolk, the printer of an anarchistic magazine, at a demonstration. Stolk and his girlfriend moved in with Van Duijn and his girlfriend. At this address, they printed the first Provo magazine. The police immediately raided the apartment and confiscated the magazines.

465 SPEAKERS' CORNER VONDELPARK

Vondelpark

Provo had a huge effect but it ended in May 1967, only two years after Roel van Duijn gave the movement its name, when Robert Jasper Grootveld and Rob Stolk declared provo dead during a meeting at speakers' corner in Vondelpark. Provo, known for their funny, disruptive actions, had become a mannerism and even institutionalised (they even had a seat on the city council), they said. It was time to bury the movement.

5 places about

WORLD WAR II

466 HOLLANDSCHE SCHOUWBURG

Plantage
Middenlaan 24
Plantage Q ②
+31 (0)20 531 03 10
*www.hollandsche
schouwburg.nl*

The Nazis made the Hollandse Schouwburg, a popular theatre built in 1892, a playhouse for Jews only. From 1942 onwards, Jews gathered here before they were deported to concentration camps throughout Europe. The theatre is now a documentation centre about the Holocaust. The building has a wall listing 6700 Jewish family names commemorating the 104.000 Dutch Jews killed during the war.

467 HOMOMONUMENT

Keizersgracht /
Westermarkt
Old Centre ①
*www.homo
monument.nl*

It's easy to miss the monument for gays and lesbians killed by the Nazis. The monu-ment, which was inaugurated in 1987, is considered to be the first of its kind in the world. The triangle-shaped lines on the ground refer to the pink triangles gays had to wear in concentration camps. One of the angles points at the Anne Frank House, another to the former headquarters of a gay organisation at Rozenstraat 14.

468 JEWISH HISTORICAL MUSEUM

Nieuwe Amstel-
straat 1
Plantage Q ②
+31 (0)20 531 03 10
www.jhm.nl

The Jewish Historical Museum opened in 1932 in Nieuwmarkt, but was forced to close during the war. Much of its collection was looted. Currently, the museum is located in the former synagogue complex in Jonas Daniël Meijerplein. It has a permanent exhibition about the history and culture of the Jews in the Netherlands, and temporary (art) exhibitions which are often positively surprising.

469 DOKWERKER

Jonas Daniël
Meijerplein
Plantage Q ②

The Nazis barred the Jews that lived in occupied Amsterdam from many public places, shops and cafes. On Monday evening, 24 February 1941, representatives from the illegal communist party addressed a small crowd about resisting the oppression. A strike started one day later, which spread through the city and lasted for two days. Nine people were killed, many more injured, and 300 communists were arrested. In 1952, this monument was inaugurated.

470 WOLKERS' AUSCHWITZ MONUMENT

Wertheimpark
Plantage Q ②

The monument of the writer and artist Jan Wolkers to commemorate the horrors of Auschwitz was inaugurated in 1993. The broken mirrors reflect heaven day and night, Wolkers said. 'Heaven is damaged for good. It's a God-awful assault on everything human'. A commemoration of the victims of Auschwitz is organised every year on 27 January, the day on which the Russian army liberated the camp.

5 *famous*

SQUATTED BUILDINGS

---

471 **OT301**

Overtoom 301
West ④
+31 (0)20 412 29 54
www.ot301.nl

The former Film Academy at Overtoom 301 was squatted in 1999. A group of artists demanded affordable studios for artists and wanted to give the vacant building a public purpose. OT301 organises concerts and parties, exhibitions, and shows cult and art films in a small movie theatre. There is also a vegan restaurant.

472 **DE NIEUWE ANITA**

Frederik Hendrik-
straat 111
West ④
www.denieuweanita.nl

In July 1983, squatters moved into Frederik Hendrikschool, a vacant domestic science school. They bought the building in 1989. The building now accommodates the cafe and music venue De Nieuwe Anita, as well as organisations that help refugees and addicts.

473 **OCCII**

Amstelveenseweg 134
South ⑥
+31 (0)20 671 77 78
www.occii.org

This former horse tram garage was squatted in 1984 and became a cultural complex known as De Binnenpret. There is a vegan and vegetarian restaurant (Eerste Schinkelstraat 16) here as well as a political bookshop and a children's theatre. The eye-catcher is the concert venue OCCII.

474 VRANKRIJK

Spuistraat 216
Old Centre ②
www.vrankrijk.org

Spuistraat is a popular place in the city centre. But it wasn't always like this. The street was completely run-down in the eighties and many buildings were under threat from demolition. Several of them were squatted. Most of the squatters were evicted in recent years. Only Vrankrijk, an old printing house that was squatted in 1982, is still squatted today. It still has living spaces and a cafe.

475 FILMHUIS CAVIA

Van Hallstraat 52-1
Westerpark Q ④
+31 (0)20 681 14 19
www.filmhuiscavia.nl

Filmhuis Cavia opened after Prinses Beatrix Schippersinternaat, a vacant boarding school, was squatted in 1983. This tiny underground art cinema (40 seats) programmes movies from all over the world on a range of topics. The rest of the building is used by artists and a kickboxing school.

473 OCCII

5 world-famous
AMSTERDAMMERS

476 JOHAN CRUYFF

Akkerstraat 32
Watergraafsmeer ⑤

Johan Cruijff (1947-2016) was one of the best football players of all time, but he also enriched the Dutch language with some widely used 'Cruijfian' language. 'Every advantage has its disadvantage', for instance. Cruijf was born in Betondorp at Akkerstraat 32, where his parents had a greengrocer's. The former Ajax stadium De Meer was located across the street in Middenweg.

477 ANNE FRANK

THE SECRET ANNEX

Prinsengracht
263-267
Old Centre ①

As a 4-year-old, Anne Frank (1929-1945) moved from Germany to Amsterdam. The family initially lived in Merwedeplein, where a monument was erected in 2005. They went into hiding in 1942, in what became widely known as Het Achterhuis (The Secret Annex). Anne died in the concentration camp of Bergen-Belsen. Her diary became so popular after the war that plans to demolish the Achterhuis were cancelled.

478 REMBRANDT VAN RIJN
RIJKSMUSEUM
Museumstraat 1
Museum Q ③

Rembrandt van Rijn's (1606-1669) greatest masterpiece The Night Watch is on display in the Rijksmuseum as well as several other works by the artist. But don't forget to pay a visit to his house and studio at Jodenbreestraat 4, where the painter lived and worked from 1639 till 1658. The Rembrandt House also organises temporary exhibitions in this two-storey dwelling.

479 HERMAN BROOD
CAFÉ DE TOOG
Nicolaas Beetsstraat 142
West ④
www.cafedetoog.com

Herman Brood (1946-2001) lived at the corner of Jan van Eyckstraat and Memlingstraat, until he committed suicide by jumping off the Hilton Hotel around the corner. In addition to being a rock 'n' roll musician, Brood was an enthusiastic painter. He painted canvasses, but also blinds, boats and busses. In Café De Toog, where Brood was a regular since it opened in 1990, he painted several tables.

480 ANNIE M.G. SCHMIDT
CEMETERY ZORGVLIED
Amsteldijk 273
South ⑥

A lot of Dutch children grew up with Annie M.G. Schmidt's (1911-1995) books Mick and Mandy, Tow-Truck Pluck and Abeltje. She also wrote poems and songs for people all ages. Schmidt started out as a journalist for the Amsterdam daily Het Parool. She lived outside of Amsterdam for most of her life, but her characters and locations are often inspired by her experiences in the city. Schmidt is buried in Zorgvlied Cemetery.

5 people
WHO BUILT AMSTERDAM

———————

481 FLOOR WIBAUT

Wibautstraat
Oosterpark Q ⑤

As Amsterdam's first socialist alderman, Floor Wibaut (1859-1936), 'the Mighty', replaced shoddy hovels and dank basement apartments with clean, tidy and beautiful workers' homes. He believed that affordable housing for poor families should be subsidised. Amsterdam became a paragon of social housing, a title that it still holds today, although the percentage of social housing is rapidly diminishing.

482 HENDRIK PETRUS BERLAGE

Victorieplein
South ③

At the start of the 20th century, the architect H.P. Berlage (1856-1934) was asked to plan a southern extension to the city. Plan Zuid is internationally renowned for its geometrical and monumental character. The houses were designed by 17 architects of the so-called Amsterdam School of architecture. Berlage, who had already designed the Beurs van Berlage, also created the Berlage Bridge over the Amstel river. You can see a huge statue of him, made by the famous sculptor Hildo Krop, in Victorieplein.

483 PIERRE CUYPERS
Central Station
Old Centre ②

There are two buildings you can hardly miss in Amsterdam: the city's Central Station and the Rijksmuseum. Both were designed by Pierre Cuypers (1827-1921). He was the first Dutch architect with an international reputation, but not free of criticism. Some considered his neo-Gothic and Renaissance style to be 'kitsch'. Cuypers also designed over 100 churches, of which Vondelkerk and Posthoornkerk are just two fine examples.

484 HILDO KROP
Erasmuspark
West ④

If you haven't seen Hildo Krop (1884-1970), then you haven't seen Amsterdam. This sculptor created over 400 works for the city, from small ornaments on bridges and buildings, to massive statues such as the *Berlage* statue (Victorieplein) and *Girl and horse* (Muzenplein). Closer to the city centre, you can see his animals on bridges over the canals. Once you recognise his style, Hildo Krop is hard to miss.

485 ALDO VAN EYCK
GARDEN OF THE
RIJKSMUSEUM
Museumstraat 1
Museum Q ③

After WWII, both the number of children and cars in the city dramatically increased. Amsterdam needed places where children could play safely. Aldo van Eyck (1918-1999) designed between 700 and 900 playgrounds all over Amsterdam, made of concrete and aluminium. Nowadays his playgrounds are considered too dangerous for children, and only a few are left. The Rijksmuseum has a genuine Van Eyck. It's in the garden.

5 places to experience
AMSTERDAM'S
GOLDEN AGE

486 WEST-INDISCH HUIS
Herenmarkt 99
Haarlemmer Q ①

From 1626 till 1656 this was the headquarters of the Dutch West India Company. This trading company played an important role in the Dutch slave trade: it was here that the decision was made to trade in slaves, as well as in sugar, tobacco and gold. A decade earlier, in 1625, the Dutch West India Company decided to build a fort on the island of Manhattan, which became New-Amsterdam or present-day New York.

487 TRIPPENHUIS
Kloveniers-
burgwal 29
Old Centre ②

This imposing Classicist building used to house the Rijksmuseum but today it is where the members of The Royal Netherlands Academy of Arts and Sciences meet. It was built in 1662 for the brothers Louys and Hendrick Trip, two iron and arms traders. During the Eighty Years' War, they supplied Spain with arms. Louys Trip later became a mayor of Amsterdam and the chairman of The Dutch East India Company.

488 STADSBANK VAN LENING

Nes 57
Old Centre ②
www.amsterdam.nl/sbl

In the 17th century, Amsterdam was bursting out of its seams as the population had tripled between 1578 and 1622. But not everyone was wealthy. To get by, people pawned their possessions at the municipal pawnbroker. The 'Stadsbank van Lening' was founded in 1614 and is still in business. Admitting to poverty was quite shameful at the time: the Stadbank's entrance was called 'the doorstep of shame'.

489 HUIS DE PINTO

Sint Antoniesbree-
straat 69
Old Centre ②
+31 (0)20 370 02 10
www.huisdepinto.nl

The De Pinto House almost had to make way for a four-lane motorway in the 1970s, but it was saved from demolition and now houses a cultural centre. It was built in 1605 and was later bought by the Portuguese-Jewish De Pinto merchant family. The classicist facade conceals an opulently decorated interior with several original ceiling paintings.

490 ROYAL PALACE AMSTERDAM

Dam
Old Centre ②
+31 (0)20 620 40 60
*www.paleis
amsterdam.nl*

When the palace was built in 1655, it was the biggest town hall in the world. In 1808, it became a royal palace when Louis Napoleon decided to make it his palace. Later, Dutch monarchists presided here. The proclamation for Dutch Independence was signed here in 1813, as well as the Independence of Indonesia in 1949. Nowadays, the palace is partly opened as a museum.

5 words in
AMSTERDAM DIALECT

---

491 MESJOGGE

Bargoens is a form of Dutch slang used in the 17th century by travelling salesmen, vagrants and criminals. It has borrowed a lot of words from Yiddish and Hebrew, and over the years has become part of our language. You can still hear many of these words in Amsterdam, although fewer and fewer people use them. *Mesjogge* is Yiddish and means crazy, foolish or lunatic.

492 ACHENEBBISJ

If something looks really run down, shabby and poor, you would call it *achenebbisj*. In the 1980s, this term applied to a lot of inner city neighbourhoods in Amsterdam, when people fled the city, and buildings were run down, for instance in the area around Central Station, Zeedijk and parts of the Jordaan and Haarlemmerdijk quarters.

493 GEINPONUM

A *geinponum* is someone who thinks he's funny. Someone who makes obvious, unsubtle jokes. Some people will be annoyed by this, but others love it. You can still find typically Amsterdam *geinponum* in pubs, at markets or even in the tram. Just politely smile when a *geinponum* cracks a cheesy joke at you.

494 ATENOJE

An exclamation of surprise. When you see something strange or unexpected, you say *Atenoje!* It's equivalent to 'My god!', and stems from the Hebrew Adonai meaning My lord. So, next time someone almost runs you over in the street with their bike, yell *Atenoje!*

495 PIKKETANUSSIE

A *pikketanussie* is slang for a stiff drink, usually jenever. Johnny Jordaan (1924-1989), one of Amsterdam's most famous Amsterdam torch song singers, used to sing: 'a piketanussie always goes down well'. Jenever has been a popular spirit since the 18th century. Robert Hennebo wrote in his Praise for Jenever (1718): 'A jenever in the morning is refreshing and makes you healthy'.

5

FILMS

featuring Amsterdam

---

496 THE FAULT IN OUR STARS
Leidsegracht 4
Canal Belt South ③

The bench before the house at Leidsegracht 4 suddenly disappeared following the success of *The Fault in Our Stars*. It's the place where Hazel and Gus talked and kissed each other along Amsterdam's canals. Nobody knew what happened to the bench, but the municipal government didn't rule out that a fan had taken it. The municipality replaced the bench in the summer of 2014.

497 AMSTERDAMNED
Canal Belt South ③

The Dutch director Dick Maas' *Amsterdamned* (1988) is a cult classic about a psychopath in the Amsterdam Canals. The detective Eric Visser, played by Huub Stapel, is tasked with stopping him. The movie's climax is a pursuit through the canals. Part of the chase, it must be said, was shot on the canals of the city of Utrecht.

498 TURKS FRUIT
Old Centre ②

Paul Verhoeven's *Turks Fruit* (1983) is one of the most successful Dutch films of all time. The story, after Jan Wolker's eponymous novel, is about a young sculptor called Erik who meets Olga while hitchhiking. She's the love of his life. They get married, but their luck doesn't last forever. In an iconic scene, the couple cycles through the historic city on one bike.

499 PRINS
North ⑦

Most films about Amsterdam use the picturesque canal belt as a backdrop, but not Sam de Jong's debut *Prins* (*Prince*, 2015). Instead he focused on a poor area in Amsterdam North, telling the coming-of-age story of Ayoub (15) who does everything to win a girl's attention, from buying fancy shoes to collaborating with a notorious criminal.

500 OCEAN'S TWELVE
Handboogstraat 29
Old Centre ②

This second movie about Danny Ocean and his band of master thieves is partly set in Amsterdam. George Clooney, Brat Pitt and Matt Damon meet their client in the Dampkring coffee shop at Handboogstraat 29. Another scene is set in Amsterdam Central Station. Unfortunately, it was under renovation at the time. The scene was therefore shot in Haarlem's Central Station.

INDEX

COLOPHON

EDITING *and* COMPOSING — Saskia Naafs and Guido van Eijck
GRAPHIC DESIGN — Joke Gossé and Tinne Luyten
PHOTOGRAPHY — Joram Van Holen and Tino van den Berg
COVER IMAGE — REM-Eiland (secret 54)

The addresses in this book have been selected after thorough independent
research by the authors, in collaboration with Luster Publishers. The selection
is solely based on personal evaluation of the business by the authors. Nothing
in this book was published in exchange for payment or benefits of any kind.

D/2015/12.005/9
ISBN 978 94 6058 1441
NUR 506, 511

© 2015, Luster, Antwerp
Fifth edition, March 2019 – Fifth reprint, March 2019
www.lusterweb.com – www.the500hiddensecrets.com
info@lusterweb.com

Printed in Italy by Printer Trento.

All rights reserved.
No part of this publication may be reproduced,
stored in a retrieval system, or transmitted, in any
form or by any means, without the prior written
consent of the publisher. An exception is made
for short excerpts, which may be cited for the sole
purpose of reviews.